MVFOL

CINDERS & SM...

D0117165

A Mile by Mile Guide
for the
Durango & Silverton
Narrow Gauge Railroad

by
Doris B. Osterwald

Western Guideways, Ltd.

Publisher – Guidebooks · Railroad and Western History
PO Box 150532·Lakewood, Colorado 80215·303/237-0583

CINDERS & SMOKE

A Mile by Mile Guide®
for the
Durango and Silverton Narrow Gauge Railroad

Seventh Edition, Copyright© 1995 by Western Guideways, Ltd.
Thirty-first printing, 1998

ISBN: 0-931788-95-1

Electronic Imagesetting by:
National Teleprinting, Inc.
Denver, Colorado

Printed by:
Golden Bell Press
Denver, Colorado

Printed in the United States of America

TABLE OF CONTENTS

ACKNOWLEDGMENTS

Anniversaries are always special. They bring forth wonderful memories of years past and exciting events. I have enjoyed more than thirty years of watching and riding **The Silverton** as it winds its way along the Animas River between Durango and Silverton. It is most rewarding to have written a book that remains popular after all these years. My abiding thanks to each and every reader.

In addition to the thrill of listening to a steam engine laboring up a steep grade, the melodious sound of a whistle echoing across a canyon, or the dubious delight of having cinders and smoke land on my face, the people met and the friends made are very special. The list grows with each passing year.

As always, my heartfelt thanks to my family for their constant support and help in preparing this Seventh Edition. A very special thanks to son Carl, who meticulously redrafted all the maps on the computer, and insisted they should be in color.

I am fortunate to count D&SNG conductor, Richard Millard, and former engineer, Jeff Johnson, as special railroading friends. They devoted many hours to checking the guide to make sure all locations are accurate and offered suggestions to make this edition more complete and interesting. Longtime friend, D&SNG vice president, Amos Cordova, graciously read the text and encouraged me in this revision. A special thanks to my dear friend, Jack Thode. His help, advice, and support through the years have been invaluable. Thanks also to Larry Bell, president of Golden Bell Press, and his fine staff, for their assistance during the past fourteen years. One of the tedious chores in completing a manuscript involves proofreading and editing. My thanks to Joan White, with Executive Editors, for her careful and thoughtful suggestions and corrections.

The magnificent San Juan Mountains are among my favorite Colorado locations. In addition to their beauty, I find their history fascinating. Each year additional facts about the area are unearthed; a few are included in this edition. A primary source of information on the earliest white settlers in the Animas Canyon, which has been painstakingly documented by Allen Nossaman, is his wonderful series, *Many More Mountains*. For those interested in all facets of Colorado history, Duane Smith's many books are invaluable resources.

It's been a fantastic thirty years!

—DBO, July 1995

4

INTRODUCTION

Welcome aboard the Durango & Silverton Narrow Gauge Railroad. You are about to embark on an unforgettable narrow gauge steam rail journey along the spectacular and ever-changing Animas River. This somewhat nostalgic means of transportation is a relic of earlier times. If the first few flakes of placer gold had not been discovered at Silverton in 1860-61, and if the Denver & Rio Grande Railway had not decided to expand its narrow gauge system to the growing mining camp along the Animas River, your trip would not be possible today.

The Silverton generally follows the Animas River as it meanders back and forth across the lovely lower valley. But the slow-moving character of the river changes beyond Baker's Bridge to that of a river running wild through an almost inaccessible gorge. Past the gorge, the track continues to follow the rushing, tumbling Animas to Silverton. The distinctive greenish color of the water probably is due to copper salts from mines surrounding Silverton.

Beyond Rockwood, the only access to the canyon is by train, foot, horseback, kayak, or raft. Your train will not be whistling for any highway crossings! The remote and incredibly beautiful, glacially-carved peaks and cirque basins of the Weminuche Wilderness are visible from the train—if you look up. These 13,000 to 14,000 ft (3,900 to 4,200 m) mountain peaks are some of the most rugged and inaccessible of any in Colorado. As your train labors up grade, you may not be aware that these awesome, towering peaks stand at least one mile above the bottom of the canyon. Each mile of your journey brings forth vistas of the majestic snow-capped peaks, small, secluded mountain parks, vertical avalanche tracks, and the remains of former mines, all of which make for a memorable experience.

When gold was discovered in Colorado in 1859, only fine particles and flakes were recovered with placer mining. After more complex ores were located in lode deposits, it was necessary to separate the gold from worthless rock, using arrastras and stamp mills (see p. 95), before it could be shipped to eastern smelters. Pack trains could carry only the richest ores across the mountains on narrow, indistinct trails that had been used by animals and Indians for centuries. As new strikes were made, mining camps sprang up almost overnight. Trails gradually were improved and became narrow, rutted roads. Freight wagons, pulled by oxen or mules, made slow, laborious trips back and forth carrying ore, mining machinery, and other essentials to the growing communities.

By June 1870, when the Denver Pacific Railroad chugged into Denver from Cheyenne, Wyoming, mining camps all over Colorado starting dreaming of rail service to link their infant towns with Denver. The Denver Pacific connected with the recently completed transcontinental Union Pacific

Railroad at Cheyenne. Railroads could carry passengers, heavy mining machinery, equipment, coal, lumber, ores, and other freight more efficiently than pack trains or wagons. Profits from such operations were expected to pay for construction and leave handsome dividends for stockholders.

The Denver & Rio Grande Railway Company (D&RG) was incorporated in the Territories of Colorado and New Mexico October 27, 1870, to build a railroad from Denver south to El Paso, Texas. The company also planned to extend rails to Mexico City, Mexico. The route to El Paso was to go south to Pueblo, west through the Arkansas River Canyon (Royal Gorge), across Poncha Pass and into the San Luis Valley to the Rio Grande River. Tracks were to follow the Rio Grande southward to El Paso. Six branches were planned to the mining areas of Colorado, and one branch was projected to reach Salt Lake City, Utah. The San Juan Extension was to be built to Silverton, a booming mining town in the San Juans. The route selected meandered back and forth along the Colorado-New Mexico border, past easily available coal and timber supplies, in which the Rio Grande invested and developed. President of this first narrow gauge railroad in Colorado was General William Jackson Palmer, who served in the Civil War with distinction and came west after the war to work on the Kansas Pacific Railroad. This line reached Denver August 15, 1870.

The Rio Grande decided to build its railroad "narrow gauge" (rails 3 ft apart) rather than "standard gauge" (rails 4 ft, 8   in apart) which was the standard on most other U.S. railroads. The choice was made because narrow gauge construction was cheaper: equipment cost less, and sharper curves were possible. Thus, it was better adapted to mountainous terrain. The railroad was only 11 years old when Palmer and his associates realized they were bucking great odds with a narrow gauge main line operation. Consequently, by late 1890, the main line to Salt Lake City, via Leadville and Tennessee Pass, was converted to standard gauge. Portions of the original main line to Salt Lake City across Marshall Pass and through Gunnison, Colorado, remained narrow gauge until abandonment in 1955. Standard gauge rail was laid to Antonito in 1901, thus dual gauging a portion of the original San Juan Extension.

The San Juan Extension managed to survive until the late 1960s, but **The Silverton** was the only portion of the route that showed a profit, as tourists and railfans discovered the pleasure of a leisurely rail journey along the Animas River to Silverton. In 1968, the Interstate Commerce Commission approved the abandonment of the narrow gauge between Antonito and Durango. Through the efforts of many individuals, preservation societies and towns, the Colorado-New Mexico Railroad Authorities were organized, and by July 1970, the two states purchased the line between gauge operates as the Cumbres & Toltec Scenic Railroad (C&TS). The other portions of the San Juan Extension were abandoned in 1970.

On June 1, 1967, the National Park Service designated the Silverton Branch of the D&RGW Railroad as a National Historical Landmark. In March 1968, the Silverton Branch also was designated as a National Historic Civil Engineering Landmark by the American Society of Civil Engineers. This award recognizes the tremendous part played by the civil engineering profession in surveying and constructing the branch through the difficult winter and spring of 1881-82. Then, on July 11, 1982, the National Railway Historical Society dedicated a beautiful granite monument at Cascade Canyon Wye. This dedication was made exactly one hundred years after passenger service commenced on the Silverton Branch of the San Juan Extension (p. 143).

The D&RG experienced years of financial turmoil and bankruptcy proceedings, and in 1921 it was reorganized as Denver & Rio Grande Western Railroad (D&RGW). The D&RGW continued to operate the Silverton Branch as an isolated segment of its once vast narrow gauge system until 1981, when the line was purchased by Charles E. Bradshaw, Jr., and renamed the Durango & Silverton Narrow Gauge Railroad (D&SNG). Included in the sale were steam locomotives, buildings, rolling stock, roadbed, and work equipment. The D&SNG has expanded passenger service from the former two trains per day operated by the D&RGW to at least four daily excursion trains during the busy summer months.

In March 1997 the D&SNG was sold to First American Railways, Inc., headquartered in Hollywood, Florida.

When the Silverton Branch opened for business in July 1882, those first travelers probably never would have thought it possible that 100 years later more than 200,000 people would travel along the same route each year. One wonders if those early passengers were as awestruck by the incredible beauty of this remote canyon surrounded by the magnificent peaks of the Needle Mountains and the Grenadier Range as are today's visitors.

USING THE MILE BY MILE GUIDE®

The Mile by Mile Guide® describes scenic highlights and points of interest along the railroad and is keyed to mileposts and U.S. Forest Service signs near the track. Nine guide maps are included that illustrate the railroad route in sections. The Index Map on page 9 shows the Durango-Silverton region and the positions of the overlapping guide maps.

The mileposts are numbered signs, visible from two directions, on slender steel posts (see photo on back cover) that are spaced one mile apart along the *east* side of the track. Numbers on the mileposts indicate the distance by rail from Denver, where the D&RG started in 1870. Thus, at the time the railroad was built, there were 451.5 miles of track from Denver to the Durango depot, and 496.7 miles to the Silverton depot.

To aid in locating the points of interest on the guide maps, the railroad route is drawn with cross-ties ¹⁄₁₀ mile apart. Entries in the guide text show the mileage at each point to the nearest ¹⁄₂₀ of a mile.

GEOLOGIC SYMBOLS:

Patterns in a light-tan color are used indicate different geologic formations on the guide maps. Names of the formations use the standard geologic abbreviations listed below. The upper-case letter indicates the age of the formation, while the lower-case lettering is geologic shorthand for the name of the formation or rock unit. The formations are explained in greater detail in the Columnar Section, pp. 90-91.

Quaternary Period:
Qal   Alluvium, gravel, boulders, soils along streams
Qg   Terrace gravels
Qls   Landslides; loose rocks and soil that have moved downhill
Qm   Moraines; loose rock debris left by retreating glaciers

Tertiary Period:
Ti   Quartz monzonite porphyry and other intrusive volcanic rocks
Tv   Extrusive volcanic rocks

Cretaceous Period:
Kmv   Mesaverde Group of sedimentary rocks
Km   Mancos Shale
Kd   Dakota Sandstone

Jurassic Period:
J   A number of sedimentary formations grouped together

Upper Triassic and Permian Periods:
R   Redbeds of the Dolores, Cutler, and Rico Formations

Pennsylvanian Period:
Ph   Hermosa Group
Pm   Molas Formation

Upper Devonian Period:
D   Ouray and Elbert Formations

Upper Cambrian Period:
€i   Ignacio Quartzite

Precambrian Period:
p€g   Granite
p€u   Uncompahgre Formation
p€gb   Gabbro
p€sg   Ancient schists, gneisses

INDEX MAP

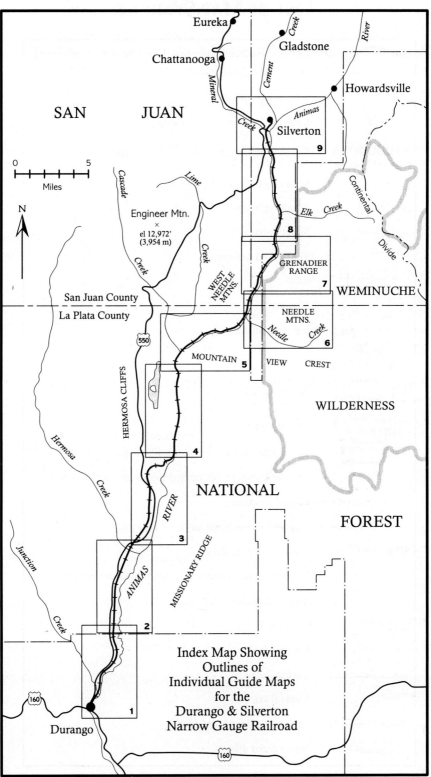

Eureka

Gladstone

Chattanooga

Howardsville

SAN   JUAN

Silverton

9

0 — 5

Miles

N

Mineral

Cement   *Creek*

Creek

Animas

Cascade

Lime

Continental

Engineer Mtn.
×
el 12,972'
(3,954 m)

Creek

Elk Creek

8

Divide

Creek

WEST
NEEDLE
MTNS.

GRENADIER
RANGE

7

WEMINUCHE

San Juan County

NEEDLE
MTNS.

La Plata County

6

550

Needle

Creek

MOUNTAIN   **5**   VIEW   CREST

HERMOSA CLIFFS

WILDERNESS

Hermosa

4

Creek

NATIONAL

FOREST

RIVER

Junction

3

MISSIONARY RIDGE

ANIMAS

2

Creek

Index Map Showing
Outlines of
Individual Guide Maps
for the
Durango & Silverton
Narrow Gauge Railroad

160

1

Durango

160

LIST OF MAP SYMBOLS

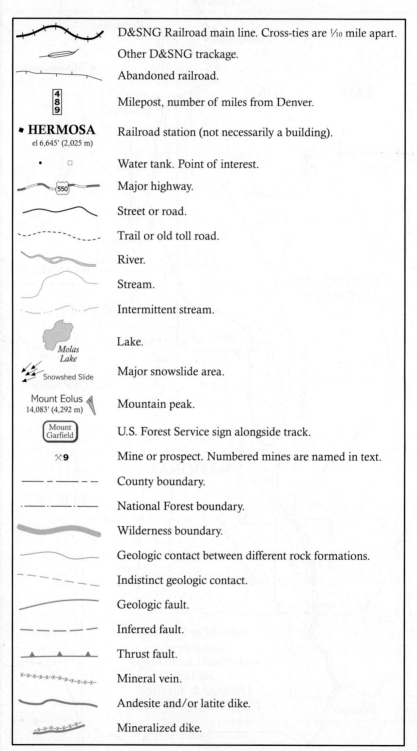

D&SNG Railroad main line. Cross-ties are ¹⁄₁₀ mile apart.

Other D&SNG trackage.

Abandoned railroad.

Milepost, number of miles from Denver.

Railroad station (not necessarily a building).

Water tank. Point of interest.

Major highway.

Street or road.

Trail or old toll road.

River.

Stream.

Intermittent stream.

Lake.

Major snowslide area.

Mountain peak.

U.S. Forest Service sign alongside track.

Mine or prospect. Numbered mines are named in text.

County boundary.

National Forest boundary.

Wilderness boundary.

Geologic contact between different rock formations.

Indistinct geologic contact.

Geologic fault.

Inferred fault.

Thrust fault.

Mineral vein.

Andesite and/or latite dike.

Mineralized dike.

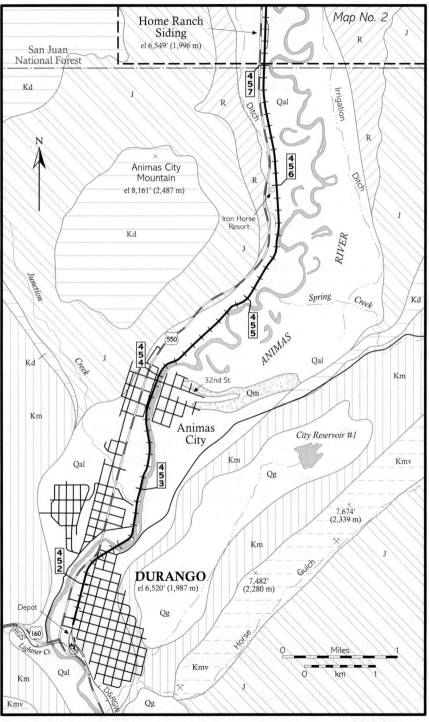

Map No. 2

Home Ranch
Siding
el 6,549' (1,996 m)

San Juan
National Forest

Kd

J

R

Qal

Irrigation

Ditch

R

R

Ditch

J

N

Animas City
Mountain
el 8,161' (2,487 m)

R

Kd

Iron Horse
Resort

J

RIVER

Spring

Creek

Kd

Junction

Creek

J

Kd

550

32nd St.

ANIMAS

Qal

Km

Km

Qm

Animas
City

City Reservoir #1

Km

Kmv

Qal

Qg

7,674'
(2,339 m)

Km

J

DURANGO
el 6,520' (1,987 m)

7,482'
(2,280 m)

Gulch

Depot

RGS

160

Lightner Cr.

Qg

Horse

Km

Qal

Kmv

J

Miles

0   1

0   km   1

Kmv

D&RGW

Qg

452

453

454

455

456

457

Map No. 1

11

MILE BY MILE GUIDE®

451.5 DURANGO DEPOT.

Elev. 6,520 ft (1,987 m)

Durango has been a railroad town since July 27, 1881, when the first D&RG construction train pulled into the new "town." Whistles, bells and a cheering crowd greeted the train at the site of the present depot. Even before track layers reached Durango, grading crews were working north toward Silverton on the last link of the D&RG Railway between Denver and the silver camp along the upper reaches of the Animas River. Only 45 miles were left to build, but what a challenge those miles proved to be! Yet, the Silverton Branch was completed in just eleven months. Men not working on the grade and track started building the depot, which was completed in January 1882. So today, as you leave on a memorable railroad journey along the Animas River, tip your hat to those undaunted builders of more than 100 years ago.

About 30 minutes before the final call, the engine puffs off the ready track near the roundhouse, rolls north across College Drive (6th Street), is switched onto the track of waiting coaches, and backs down to the train. A gentle (?) bump or two indicate the engine is coupled. The conductor gives the "All Aboard" call and your train starts to roll, crosses College Drive and goes north along Narrow Gauge Avenue.

Each D&SNG train has a normal crew complement of five. In the cab of the locomotive are the engineer and fireman. The engineer sits on the right side of the cab (facing forward) and is in charge of operating the locomotive. The fireman sits on the left side of the cab and will hand stoke the fire throughout the day, shoveling three to four tons of coal into the firebox, one shovelful at a time. The conductor is responsible for the safety of the train and its passengers, and is assisted by a head brakeman and a rear brakeman. If you have any questions not answered in this book, a member of the crew will be happy to help you.

452 CROSS 11TH STREET.

In the lively 1880s, Durango's sporting houses were west of the track on 10th and 11th Streets. The "shady ladies" houses had such names as Bessie's, Jennie's, Mattie's, the Variety Theater, Clipper, Silver Bell, and the Hanging Gardens of Babylon.

On the western skyline is Perins Peak (photo, p. 75), named for Charles Perin who surveyed the Durango townsite.

452.25 CROSS MAIN AVENUE.

Picking up speed, the engine whistles loud and clear at this crossing.

12

Cinders and smoke will become a part of your day as you follow the Mile by Mile Guide®.

Mile
452.4   CROSS ANIMAS RIVER.

This 253-ft bridge has been rebuilt several times. It consists of a steel plate girder span brought from the Pleasant Valley Branch in Utah in 1927, a steel Pratt truss span built in 1888 and brought from the Conejos River near Antonito, in 1917, and a wooden open-deck truss span built in 1936. The original bridge, built in 1881, was partially washed away during a spring flood in 1885.

A state fish hatchery, west of the track, is open to visitors every day. Started as a private hatchery, it was purchased by the state about 1900.

The houses to the east are on an outwash terrace (or plain) of loose gravel, sand, boulders, and soil deposited by meltwater streams flowing from a terminal moraine located almost two miles north (Map No. 1). A terminal or end moraine is a mound or ridge that marks the farthest advance of a glacier. Behind the terrace is a cliff of soft gray-to-black Mancos Shale, which was deposited as mud in a sea some 90 million years ago.

A nice view of the La Plata Mountains is to the northwest. On the western skyline is another view of Perins Peak. It is capped with tan-to-rusty brown sandstone ledges of the Mesaverde Group that were deposited near the shore of an old sea. The Boston Coal & Fuel Co. opened a coal mine on the western side of Perins Peak in 1901. The Rio Grande Southern Railroad operated a privately-built branch to the mine and town which had a steady 4.5% grade and very sharp curves. The mine operated until 1926.

Mile
452.9   CROSS JUNCTION CREEK.

This stream flows into the Animas River from the northwest. The bridge was completely rebuilt during the winter of 1992.

Milepost
453   TRACK ALONG ANIMAS RIVER.

Wildflowers include Rocky Mountain iris, sand lilies, tiny white daisies, and the ever-present dandelions in the spring; primroses, locoweed, sunflowers, and harebells in the summer months, and purple asters, yellow composites, and cattails in the fall.

Mile
453.9   CROSS 32ND STREET.

This is the site of ANIMAS CITY, settled in 1874. Postal service was available from February 1877 until September 1900. When the D&RG decided to follow the Animas River to Silverton, railroad officials visited Animas City and proposed to build a depot and yards at Animas City if the town would cooperate by donating a right-of-way and depot site, help with grading through town and perhaps purchase some railroad stock. Animas City declined the offer and the company town of Durango was laid out two miles below the struggling farming community. Grading was completed to Animas City July 20, 1881, but track did not reach the town until October 1, 1881. Soon, most businesses moved to Durango, and Animas City became a northern suburb. In 1947, the town was annexed to the city of Durango.

To the east are sinuous, low, hummocky hills of glacial debris that represent the signature of a terminal moraine. During Pleistocene time, starting about 10,000 years ago, the Animas Glacier, the largest in the San Juan Mountains, flowed as far south as Animas City. Here it stopped, deposited its load of sand, gravel, and boulders, and gradually receded to the high mountain cirques north and northwest of Silverton. These rounded irregular hills are best seen on the return trip.

Mile
454.7   TRAILER PARK.

The cliffs on the western skyline above the trailer park are thick, rusty-brown, and light tan layers of the Dakota Sandstone (Kd on map) at the top, which were deposited as sand in a sea about 100 million years ago. Below the Dakota Sandstone are multicolored shales, mudstones, and sandstones of the Morrison Formation, which were deposited as sand and mud by rivers and lakes about 150 million years ago. The base of the cliffs is massive, white-to-buff sandstone of the Entrada Formation, which was deposited by wind in ancient dunes about 160 million years ago. The Morrison and Entrada are shown together on maps as J.

As your train continues up the valley, the tilted sedimentary rocks gradually disappear beneath the surface. These same rocks are deeply buried in the San Juan Basin of northern New Mexico. Between Durango and Rockwood, the route passes sedimentary rocks that represent about 500 million years of geologic time (Geologic Column, pp. 90-91).

Milepost
455   SHARP BEND IN RIVER CHANNEL NEAR TRACK.

The Grand Motor Car and Piano Collection Museum is on the left. Established in 1992, the museum houses a fine collection of pianos and classic automobiles valued at more than $2 million. Open daily.

The buff-colored sandstone cliff above U.S. 550 and also across the valley is the Entrada Formation, included in unit J on Map No. 1. These rocks dip beneath the surface opposite mile 455.5. To the north are the first views of Permian and Upper Triassic redbeds (labeled R on maps).

Mile
455.9   UNITED CAMPGROUND.

This large campground is on the west side of the track.

On opening day, May 2, 1992, newly-restored engine 482 is ready to leave Durango on its first run to Silverton. Page 146 has details on the restoration of this engine.

(D.B. Osterwald)

Milepost
456   IRON HORSE RESORT.

Along here you will see more nice views of the colorful sedimentary rocks. The bright red and rusty-red shales and thin sandstone layers are the Dolores Formation, which was deposited by rivers in an ancient desert about 170 to 187 million years ago. Animas City Mountain, elev. 8,170 ft (2,490 m), is on the western skyline.

Between mileposts 454 and 465, the Animas River meanders back and forth across the flat valley floor because the low stream gradient was established by the glacier. A number of cutoff meanders and oxbow lakes were formed when the river cut new, shorter channels between narrow, looping bends (photo, p. 23).

Thick willow groves are on both sides of the track. Shrubs along here include chokecherry, snowberry, buffaloberry, and box elder. In the fall, clematis vines have a fuzz of feathery seed tails hanging on the shrubs and trees. These feathery seed plumes make excellent tinder. A spark from flint or pyrite struck into a ball of the fuzz will quickly ignite. Indians also used the fuzz inside moccasins for padding and insulation.

Clematis seed plume

15

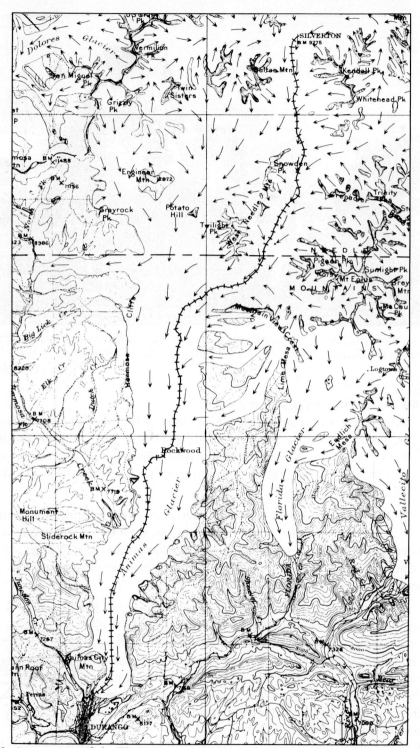

Maximum extent of the Wisconsin stage glaciers in the Animas Canyon area. After U.S. Geological Survey Professional Paper 166, plate 3.

16

457.25   HOME RANCH SIDING.

This 1,000-ft siding was built in 1982 to provide a meeting point for the additional trains that operate on the D&SNG. When rails reached this point October 20, 1881, the D&RG construction crews never dreamed a passing track at this site would be needed. Farther north, an old spur track named HOME RANCH was at mile 457.9. The siding, a cattle chute, and a wooden platform were removed many years ago.

457.5   VIEWS OF REDBEDS.

On both sides of the valley, the redbeds (R on maps) have a total thickness of about 2,500 ft. In addition to the Dolores Formation at the top, there are 1,900 ft of the Cutler Formation, and about 130 ft of the Rico Formation at the base of the valley. These redbeds were deposited as sand and mud by rivers flowing across an ancient desert about 200 million years ago. The red color formed when magnetite, an iron-bearing mineral, rusts and the resulting minerals—hematite and limonite—coated and cemented the sand grains together.

Due north is Potato Hill (locally called Spud Mountain), named for "Potato" John Raymond, a favorite cook on some early geological surveys of the West.

458.5   WATERFALL ON CLIFF TO THE WEST.

Falls Creek flows off layers of the Cutler Formation. The ranch, just east of the falls, is named "Waterfall," and is one of the oldest in the valley. It was started by Thomas H. Wigglesworth, chief construction engineer for the Silverton Branch of the D&RG. He also surveyed the branch to the Perins Peak coal mine.

Between milepost 458 and mile 459.5, herds of elk often are seen during the winter runs of the **Cascade Canyon Train**.

459   FIRST VIEW OF MOUNTAIN VIEW CREST.

This mountain range (Map No. 5, p. 44) is on the northeastern skyline. Better views are farther up the canyon.

Along both sides of the track, a wide variety of wildflowers blooms throughout the summer and fall. Silver sage, clover, butter and eggs, clematis vines, thistles, Indian paintbrush, goldenrod, and cattails are common. Cattails have many uses. The leaves are used for weaving; the brown flowers can be used for tinder in starting a fire, or in bouquets. When separated, the fuzz can be used for insulation or bedding. The lower stem and roots contain nearly pure starch that can be eaten either cooked or raw. The cores of the large rootstocks were dried and ground into meal by the Indians and early settlers. Muskrat, geese, and elk like to feed on the rootstocks and new shoots.

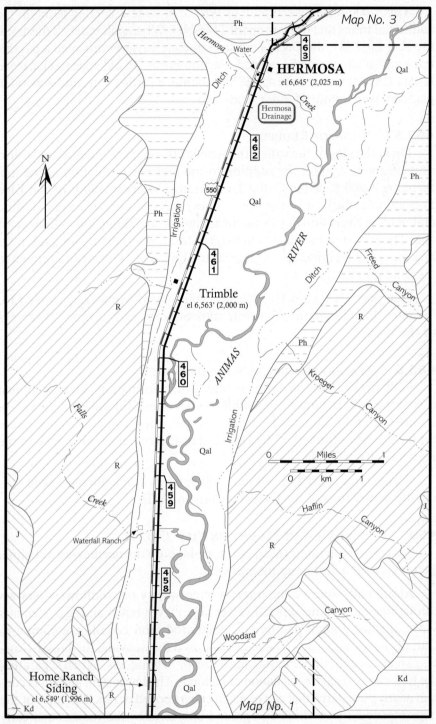

N

Ph

Hermosa

Water

🔲463

HERMOSA
el 6,645' (2,025 m)

Qal

R

Hermosa Creek

Hermosa
Drainage

🔲462

Ph

550

Qal

RIVER

Ph

🔲461

Irrigation

Ditch

Freed Canyon

Trimble
el 6,563' (2,000 m)

R

R

ANIMAS

Ph

🔲460

Kroeger Canyon

Falls

Irrigation

Qal

0   Miles   1
0   km   1

🔲459

Haflin Canyon

J

Creek

R

R

J

Waterfall Ranch

🔲458

Canyon

J

Woodard

Home Ranch
Siding
el 6,549' (1,996 m)

R

Qal

J

Kd

Kd

Map No. 2

18

Hermosa House Hotel at Trimble Hot Springs circa 1910. This peaceful scene was recorded by D&RG photographer, George L. Beam.

(D&RGW collection, courtesy Jackson C. Thode)

Mile
460.7　TRIMBLE HOT SPRINGS.
Elev. 6,563 ft (2,000 m)

A small depot with a platform was built in 1883 for excursionists who came from Durango and other towns. There was also a short siding.

William and Rufina Trimble settled near the springs in 1874. William found that the curative hot water helped his rheumatism, so in March 1882, he purchased 160 acres of land surrounding the springs for $200 and planned to built a spa. Because the Trimbles were having financial problems, the property was sold to entrepreneur T.D. Burns of Tierra Amarillo, New Mexico. The Burns family completed the first hotel and spa, which opened December 28, 1882, with a grand ball. A post office opened January 29, 1883, and lasted until September 1900.

In 1892, the first Trimble Hot Springs Hotel was destroyed by fire. The Burns family replaced the first hotel with the lavish Hermosa House Hotel in 1896. This structure lasted until July 30, 1931, when it also burned to the ground. With a change of ownership in the 1930s, a two-story pink stucco and glass-block building with a dining room and ballroom were built on the site of Hermosa House. A third fire destroyed the main building in 1963, and the resort was closed until 1988, when facilities for bath-

19

ing were rebuilt by new owners. Remarkably, the water flowing from the base of the cliff still averages 120 gallons per minute at an average temperature of 111°F.

Milepost
462   VIEWS OF ANIMAS VALLEY.
The Animas Valley from Durango to Baker's Bridge, east of milepost 466, is a broad U-shape in which the river meanders back and forth in wide sweeping curves.

Among the many wildflowers, watch for mullein, a 2-4 ft tall, coarse, woolly, spiked plant with small yellow flowers. It blooms in July. The large, coarse, olive-green leaves are velvet-like to touch, and contain chemicals used in lotions to soften the skin and in medicine to soothe inflamed tissues. Small birds eat the seeds in the dried, brown spikes when other food is covered with snow. The plant was brought to this country from Europe.

Mile
462.45   CROSS HERMOSA CREEK.
The bridge is a 64-ft long wooden Howe pony truss, installed in 1914.

Mile
462.5   HERMOSA.
     Elev. 6,645 ft (2,025 m)
A passing track and water tank are here. Locomotives are watered from a tank car body. The D&SNG keeps its maintenance-of-way equipment at this site. A wye, a frame depot and platform, section house, bunkhouse, and coal house were here many years ago. Hermosa's first settlers arrived in 1873-74. A post office was established July 27, 1876, and lasted until September 1900. Mail came via Howardsville, Silverton, and down the

Listen for one long whistle blast from the locomotive, indicating that your train is approaching Hermosa. Whenever the train approaches a designated station or flagstop, the engineer will blow one long whistle. He then will look back for instructions from the train crew, usually the head brakeman standing on the rear platform of the first coach. The brakeman will signal the engineer with either a "highball" or a "stop." A highball is a high, semicircular wave of the hand, indicating to the engineer that the train should proceed through the station without stopping. When the engineer observes a highball, he responds with two short blasts of the whistle. If the conductor has been instructed to stop the train, he will have the head brakeman single a "stop," which is a low, swinging motion of his hand. When the engineer observes this signal, he responds with three short blasts of the whistle, and then brings the train to a stop. The signal for a train to stop is one long and three short blasts. This is also the signal for the rear-end brakeman to grab his flagging kit and prepare to protect the rear of the train while it is stopped. Also note the list of whistle signals on the inside front cover.

Two views of Hermosa circa 1905-1906. The scene at the top looks northwest toward Hermosa Mountain. The bottom view looks south and shows the depot, bunkhouse, and section foreman's house. The siding at left probably has some original 30-lb rail in place, while the mainline has at least a vestige of ballast between the ties.

(W.R. Self, Center for Southwest Studies, Ft. Lewis College)

Animas Canyon, on the Animas Canyon Toll Road that was built in 1876-77. See pp. 76 and 79 for more history of the toll road. A railroad construction camp was located here after construction started from Durango. Track reached Hermosa November 1, 1881.

One of the early journalists to describe the wonders of the Silverton Branch was Ernest Ingersoll (1852-1946), who wrote for the New York *Tribune, Harper's Magazine*, and *Scribner's Monthly*. He first visited the San Juans in 1874 as a recorder for the Hayden Survey and wrote a book, *Knocking Round the Rockies*, which described his early adventures with the Survey. During the early 1880s, Ingersoll and his wife returned to Colorado, and with the blessing of S.K. Hooper, general passenger agent of the D&RG, the couple traveled on all the D&RG narrow gauge lines. A book, *Crest of the Continent,* resulted from those travels. Ingersoll described the Animas Canyon as "The Queen of the Cañons." Prior to that extensive trip, he came to Colorado in 1882 and described the construction of the Silverton Branch in the April 1882 issue of *Harper's Magazine:*

> . . .Through the bottom we could see, running straight as an arrow, the graded bed of the coming railroad, but the stage-road kept away from it until we reached the few cabins that constitute Hermosa.
>
> Presently we came upon one of Mr. Wigglesworth's construction camps—long, low buildings of logs with dirt roofs, where grasses and sunflowers and purple asters make haste to sprout, are grouped without order. Perhaps there will also be an immense tent where the crew eats. Beside the larger houses, inhabited by the engineers, foremen, etc., you will see numbers of little huts about three logs high, roofed flatly with poles, brush, and mud, and having only a window-like hole to creep in and out through; or into a sidehill will be pushed small caves with a front wall of stones or mud and a bit of canvas for a door—in these kennels the laboring men find shelter.

This is the only description of a construction camp that was found during research for this book. According to Robert W. Richardson, founder of the Colorado Railroad Museum at Golden, few construction photographs exist of early-day mountain railroads in Colorado. He believes that the builders probably did not want prospective investors and stockholders to see the terrain and methods used to build these lines, because to Easterners, the mountain construction must have seemed almost impossible. After a section of track was completed, photographers were welcome to publicize the accomplishments.

Mile
462.7   TRACK CROSSES U.S. 550.

After crossing the highway, the grade abruptly changes from 1.2% to a steady 2.5% all the way to Rockwood. Your locomotive will begin working at full throttle for the next six miles, known to D&SNG railroaders as "Hermosa Hill." Watch out—here come the cinders! The track climbs along

On May 24, 1981, the second day of operations for the new D&SNG Railroad, this double-headed train starts to climb the 2.5 percent grade to Rockwood after passing Hermosa and crossing U.S. 550. *(F.W. Osterwald)*

View northward of the Animas River valley from Animas City Mountain. Trimble Hot Springs is in the distance near the base of the western cliffs, and Hermosa is at the base of Hermosa Mountain on the left skyline. The river meanders back and forth across the flat valley floor. A number of cut-off meanders, termed ox-bow lakes, are in the foreground.

(F. Gonner, Center for Southwest Studies, Ft. Lewis College)

the west side of the valley to bypass the box canyon of the Animas above Baker's Bridge. For the next two miles, the track winds along the slope in curves that range from 12° to 24°.

Milepost
463 NICE VIEW ACROSS VALLEY.

Excellent morning photos of the lovely Animas Valley are possible along here. There are many marvelous vistas of the placid, meandering Animas River for the next several miles.

The brown, tan, and gray cliffs along the track are part of the limestone, shale and sandstone layers of the Hermosa Group (Ph on maps), about 650 ft thick. These sedimentary rocks were deposited as limy mud in a sea about 270 million years ago.

The train is beginning to climb into the timbered hills of the Piñon-Juniper Life Zone. Mullein and yucca are plentiful. The Indians made soap from yucca by pounding and pulverizing the roots. Trees along the track include low-growing dwarf junipers, Rocky Mountain junipers, some quite large Gambel (scrub) oaks, and widely spaced ponderosa pines. Gambel oak is a small tree up to 20 ft tall with shiny green leaves (photo, p. 30). Rocky Mountain Junipers are also about 20 ft tall. The needles are divided into tiny segments (like scales) and are flattened against the branchlets. The fruit is a tiny purple berry. Dwarf junipers are less than 3 ft tall and have sharp needles at the ends of the branches.

Gambel oak

Dwarf juniper

Rocky Mountain juniper

24

463.8   HONEYVILLE FARM BELOW TRACK.

Note the beekeeper's hut and sign on the east side of the track. The hives and processing plant are along U.S. Highway 550 and are open to visitors.

464.5   MISSIONARY RIDGE ACROSS VALLEY.

A logging road across the valley switches back and forth to the top of Missionary Ridge. This ridge was named by an army unit stationed in the valley in the 1870s that had fought on Missionary Ridge near Chattanooga, Tennessee, during the Civil War and had noticed a similarity of the two skylines.

465   PROMINENT GRAY TO BROWN LEDGE.

Across the valley, at the base of a cliff, is a prominent ledge of Cambrian Ignacio Quartzite, shown as €i on the map. It was deposited as sand brought to an ancient sea by rivers between 500 and 525 million years ago. The Ignacio Quartzite is the oldest sedimentary unit in the Animas Valley.

465.75   PINKERTON SIDING.

This 700-ft siding was built in 1982 as a passing track for the additional trains that now are operated by the D&SNG. For several years the westbound **Cascade Canyon Train**, Number 265, met the eastbound **Second Silverton Train**, Number 464, in the late afternoon. (You may wonder why your train, which is headed north, is referred to as the "westbound" train. This term goes back to the days of D&RG ownership, when the San Juan Extension was headed *west* from Alamosa.)

The siding is named for Judge J.H. Pinkerton, whose ranch included some hot springs. The ranch was a stop on the toll road between Silverton and Animas City. The Pinkertons were the fifth family to settle in the lower Animas valley. In August 1880, the famous Ute Chief, Ouray, stopped at the Pinkerton ranch for two days. He was ill, but continued on to Ignacio, where he died August 24, 1880. The Indians buried him near Ignacio, but kept the location a secret for 45 years.

Years later, the Pinkerton ranch became a guest ranch known as El Rancho Encatado. The property changed hands and became Pinkerton Hot Springs, and during the 1960s, the name was changed to the Golden Horseshoe Resort. Today the buildings house the Timberline Academy, a private school.

The hot springs on the property are very similar to the Trimble Springs, but the water is not as hot. The rusty, yellow-brown deposits that line the hill down to the river are travertine, deposited by the springs. The mineral water emerges along small faults that probably are parallel to the Hermosa Cliffs.

HISTORIC BAKER'S BRIDGE.

Look upstream to the north. This is the site of the first settlement in the Animas Valley. A group of prospectors, led by Captain Charles Baker (p. 71), spent the winter of 1860-61 in a cabin they built along the river. The Baker party also built the first crude log bridge across the Animas River at this location. In the years following, a few other cabins were built along the river, and the area was known as Elbert, the First Animas City, Old Animas City, or Animas City 1. A toll gate for the Animas Canyon Toll Road also was located at this site.

Milepost
466   CLIFFS ABOVE TRACK.

Brown and rusty gray limestone cliffs of the Hermosa Group are easy to see at this milepost. Gambel oaks are on both sides of the track. The shiny dark green leaves turn a lovely bronze and reddish color in the fall.

Mile
466.1   MITCHELL LAKES TRAIL CROSSING.

A popular trail for hikers and horseback riders crosses the track and heads up the hill to several small lakes (Map No. 3, p. 27). Listen for the warning whistle. A KOA Campground is below the highway.

The Durango Wheel Club's excursion to Baker's Bridge, June 16, 1895. This is undoubtedly a replacement for the first bridge built by the Baker party in 1860-61.

(F. Gonner, Pear Tree Camera Shop, Durango)

26

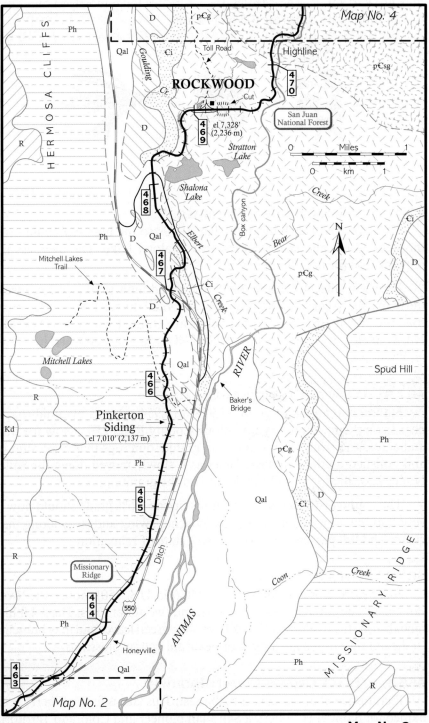

Ph

HERMOSA CLIFFS

Qal

Goulding Cr.

Ci

D

pCg

Toll Road

Highline

pCsg

ROCKWOOD

Cut

4 7 0

San Juan
National Forest

D

4 6 9

el 7,328'
(2,236 m)

Stratton
Lake

Miles

0   1

0   km   1

Shalona
Lake

Creek

4 6 8

Ph

D

Qal

Elbert

Box canyon

Bear

Ci

N

D

Mitchell Lakes
Trail

4 6 7

Ci

Creek

pCg

D

Mitchell Lakes

RIVER

Spud Hill

4 6 6

Qal

Baker's
Bridge

R

Kd

Pinkerton
Siding
el 7,010' (2,137 m)

Ph

pCg.

Ph

Qal

Ci

D

4 6 5

R

Ditch

Missionary
Ridge

Coon

Creek

MISSIONARY RIDGE

4 6 4

550

Ph

ANIMAS

Honeyville

Ph

Qal

4 6 3

Qal

Map No. 3

27

Ponderosa pine is the dominant tree. It has a reddish-brown bark and may grow to 150 ft. The needles are 3-6 inches long, mostly in bundles of two or three. The cones are 3-5 inches long.

Ponderosa pine

Milepost
467   U.S. 550 HIGHWAY OVERPASS.

This overpass was built in the late 1970s so the highway could avoid the steep grade and sharp curves near Shalona Lake. The overpass is a popular stop for rail photographers.

Between miles 466.8 and 467.8, the speed limit is 10 mph because of the many sharp curves. D&SNG railroaders call the track above the county road the "Mini High Line." These cliffs are Ouray Limestone (D on Map No. 3), which are composed of small shell fragments deposited in sea water about 330 million years ago.

Mile
467.3   VIEW OF ENGINEER MOUNTAIN.

Standing at an elevation of 12,972 ft (3,954 m), this pyramid-shaped peak is on the northern skyline. Along County Road 250, below the track and across the river, are Precambrian granite outcrops that were rounded and polished by the Animas Glacier as it slowly moved down the valley. Notice how the Ignacio Quartzite lies on the granite.

The sound of the engine as it labors up the 2.5% grade should now be very familiar. On the return trip, the coaches swing and sway along these curves and lull passengers into a drowsy state of relaxation.

Mile
467.8   OPEN HILLSIDE.

Just before crossing county road 250 (old U.S. 550), notice the lovely sloping hillside covered with rabbitbrush and sweetbriar roses. The 3-4 ft high rabbitbrush shrubs along the track have olive-green leaves and gray branches. In the fall the shrubs are a mass of beautiful yellow blossoms.

Mile
468.1   TRACK CROSSES COUNTY HIGHWAY.

Picturesque Shalona Lake is to the east. This lake is fed by Elbert Creek, named for Samuel H. Elbert, a San Juan pioneer and Colorado Territorial governor in 1873-74.

A short distance north of the highway crossing, Bell Spur and Rockwood Quarry were on the west side of the track years ago. The quarry was owned and operated by John F. Bell, who shipped limestone to a Durango smelter for use as flux.

Mile
468.5 SITE OF TRAIN WRECK.

On January 21, 1917, a special eastbound train turned over as it rounded a sharp curve, known locally as Granite Point. The newspapers of the day referred to this accident as the "Millionaire Special" because several prominent businessmen interested in purchasing the famous Sunnyside Mine (pp. 85-87) near Silverton were on board. Remarkably, none of the twenty people was seriously injured, but a fire destroyed two of the three coaches on the train when a coal stove overturned. A 10 mph slow order is required at this sharp curve.

CAMBRIAN-PRECAMBRIAN CONTACT.

This major contact (boundary) between the light-colored Cambrian Ignacio Quartzite (€i) and red coarse-grained Precambrian granite (p€g) is easy to see along the left side of the train, especially when the morning sun reflects off the mineral grains. The granite probably cooled from its molten state about 1.5 billion years ago.

Just beyond this contact, as the track curves northward and enters a small canyon along Elbert Creek, is a 24° curve. Between Hermosa and Rockwood the track has a maximum curvature of 24° and a maximum grade of 2.5% in climbing 722 ft between the two points.

Wildflowers include yucca, sumac, box elder, chokecherry, rabbitbrush, wild rose, mullein, and scarlet gilia. Many cattails line Elbert Creek.

Mile
468.9 PRIVATE POND ON WEST.

This property would be a great place to live and watch trains during the busy summer months.

Mile
469.1 ROCKWOOD.
Elev. 7,367 ft (2,245 m)

A 750-ft siding and wye are located at this flag stop. A train will not stop here unless directed to by the conductor. The tail of the wye, a track shaped like the letter Y, and used for reversing the direction of trains, has an ancient stub switch, probably the last one in use anywhere in the United States. Beyond Rockwood, there are no roads. The only access to the Animas Canyon from here to Silverton is on the train, on foot, or on horseback.

A post office was established July 8, 1876, and except for several intermittent closings, lasted until February 15, 1940. Grading and bridging crews reached Rockwood in September 1881, but track-laying was not completed

*Rockwood, Colorado in 1885. Train Number 51, the **Accomodation**, with an unidentified locomotive, is standing at the depot. Narrow gauge boxcar 3790 is sitting on the north leg of the wye. The tree stumps in the forground are in an area that was surveyed for town lots but never developed.*

(Nathan Boyce, by permission of the Colorado Railroad Museum, Golden, Colorado)

On May 26, 1981, the first narrow gauge stock extra in many years is ready to leave Rockwood with horses for Ah! Wilderness Guest Ranch. Several cars of pipe, timbers and other material for the Tacoma power plant are on the siding waiting to be moved. *(F.W. Osterwald)*

until November 26, 1881. Passenger service between Durango and Rockwood commenced in January 1882. It is difficult to believe that for a decade this location was a bustling town. During 1882, a depot, platform, section house, bunkhouse, and coal house were built. Rockwood was a popular holiday destination for picnickers from Durango and Animas City. Round trip fare was $2. See page 76 for more on the history of Rockwood (photo, p. 77).

This lovely, secluded small meadow is a delight in the spring and early summer when a multitude of wildflowers blooms.

Mile
469.2   ENTER ROCKWOOD CUT.

In 1955, this famous 350-ft cut was covered and made into a tunnel for the movie, "Around the World in 80 Days." The cut has been a favorite place for photographs since the Silverton Branch was completed.

The only *downgrade* stretch of track on the entire westbound trip to Silverton is from the northern end of Rockwood Cut to the high bridge at mile 471.2.

Mile
469.4   SAN JUAN NATIONAL FOREST SIGN.

Beside the track is an automatic wheel-flange oiler which was installed in 1981. This device reduces wear on the rail and wheel flanges.

Mile
469.5   HIGH LINE.

Have your camera ready for the spectacular views as the train snakes along the narrow shelf blasted out of red granite. The engineer has a permanent "slow order" through this gorge for safety, but also for the benefit of photographers. The water in this box canyon is more than 400 ft below the track. Wheel flanges squeak and groan, adding sound effects that are difficult to forget. Several scenes from "Butch Cassidy and the Sundance Kid" were filmed along here in 1968.

The High Line was the most difficult portion of the Silverton Branch to build. To drill into the granite walls and set the black powder shots, men had to be lowered on ropes from above. It cost about $100,000 per mile to build this narrow shelf track during the late winter and early spring of 1882.

Milepost
470   UPPER END OF SHELF TRACK.

At track level, the Central Claim was discovered in 1882. The geologic faults here contain a little gold and silver in hematite-chalcopyrite quartz veins. These faults are along the contact (or boundary) between red granite (pCg) and metamorphosed schists and gneisses (pCsg). The schists and gneisses were changed (metamorphosed) from older igneous or sedimentary rocks by extreme heat and pressure as much as 2.5 billion years ago.

Scenes from "Night Passage" and "Denver & Rio Grande" were filmed along this portion of the line.

In 1903 or 1904, Monte Ballough recorded this dramatic view of the High Line above the Animas River with the large curved trestle at mile 470.2 in the background, shortly before the trestle burned. It was replaced with a fill. Grand View Park, on the slopes above the trestle, was a popular picnic spot for excursionists who rode special trains to Rockwood. The section men at the left are on a handcar that was propelled manually by pumping the handles up and down. (Rieke's Photo Arts Studio, Durango)

*Engine 481 with the **Silverton Mixed** on the High Line, October 15, 1981. (F.W. Osterwald)*

On July 23, 1982, Silverton bound Train number 461 slowly rounds the first sharp curve along the High Line. The Cinco Animas private car (p. 124) is on the rear of the train.

(F.W. Osterwald and J.B. Bennetti, Jr.)

On December 27, 1921, this mixed train traveling to Durango hit a rock slide south of Tacoma. The head engine, 270, jumped the track, taking the flanger and engine 263 with it into the river. Fireman Hindelang jumped from the train and was not hurt, but engineer Louis Johnson was injured, and fireman John Connor was crushed to death beneath the wreckage. Both engines were repaired and remained in service many more years.

(Monte Ballough, Colorado Historical Society)

In the fall, tall tansy asters and goldenrod are abundant along the track. Tall ponderosa pines and junipers are plentiful along both sides of the valley.

Between mile 470.3 and 470.4 there was a long wooden trestle that burned in 1905. Today this area is called Overland Curve by D&SNG railroaders (photo, p. 32).

Mile
471.2   CROSS ANIMAS RIVER.
The bridge is a 130-ft wrought-iron deck-truss bridge which was built in 1880 but not installed until 1894. It was strengthened in 1981 so the heavier 480- and 490-series locomotives can safely cross the bridge.

Mile
471.3   SITE OF TRAIN WRECK.
Photographs of this accident are on page 34. Evidence of the ramp that was cut into the hillside and used to drag the wrecked engines back to track level still is visible on the west side.

The river has cut down into the granite at places of least resistance (mostly along joints and fractures in the rock) to form a narrow, post-glacial gorge. For the next six miles, the track is built on highly metamorphosed gneisses and schists of Precambrian age.

Scrub oak is still very abundant, but firs are beginning to be seen and river willows are common.

Mile
471.7   SITE OF SAVAGE.
A short spur track on the east was removed many years ago.

Mile
472.05   CANYON CREEK. CRAZY WOMAN CREEK SIGN.
Track crosses Canyon Creek. Crazy Woman Creek is actually a tributary of Canyon Creek (Map No. 4).

Mile
472.3   TACOMA.
Elev. 7,313 ft (2,229 m)

This is a flag stop. Across the river is the Tacoma Power Plant, which was completed in 1905, making it the oldest hydroelectric plant with original equipment in the U.S. Water to generate electricity comes from Electra Lake, a reservoir on Elbert Creek, 934 ft above the power plant. The water comes down the mountainside in a 66-inch pipe to Forebay Lake. From there, water descends to the power plant in three 30-inch pipes. Generator 2 was completed in 1905, and generator 1 in 1906; both produce two megawatts of power. A third generator was added in 1949, and it produces four megawatts of power. By way of comparison, one megawatt of electricity will supply power for 1,000 homes for one hour. At the time of this writing, the Public Service Co. of Colorado is upgrading the plant. Equip-

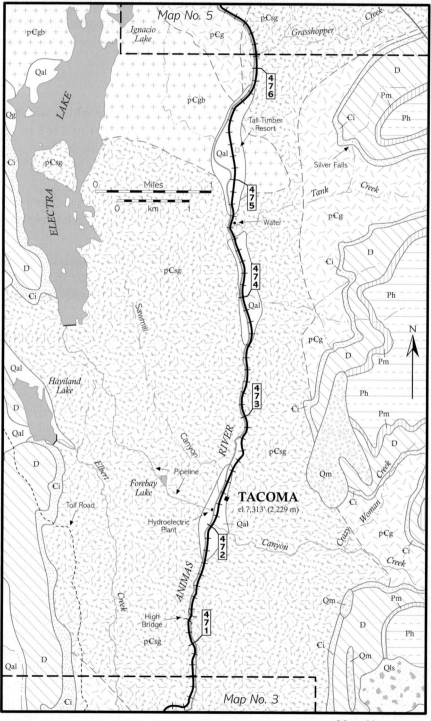

p€gb

Ignacio
Lake

p€g

p€sg

Grasshopper

Creek

Qal

LAKE

476

D

Pm

Qg

p€gb

Tall Timber
Resort

€i

Ph

€i

p€sg

ELECTRA

Qal

475

Silver Falls

Tank

Creek

0   Miles   1

0   km   1

Water

p€g

p€sg

€i

D

D

474

Ph

€i

Sawmill

Qal

p€g

D

Pm

Qal

473

Ph

Haviland
Lake

Canyon

RIVER

€i

Pm

D

Elbert

p€sg

D

Qal

D

Qm

Creek

€i

Woman

€i

Pipeline

Forebay
Lake

TACOMA
el 7,313' (2,229 m)

Qal

Crazy

p€g

Toll Road

Hydroelectric
Plant

472

Canyon

€i

Creek

Creek

ANIMAS

Qm

Pm

High
Bridge

471

D

Ph

p€sg

€i

Qm

Qal

D

Qls

€i

N

Map No. 4

36

***The Silverton**, pulled by engine 481, crosses the high bridge below Tacoma. The blow-off cocks are open to clean out the lower cavities of the boiler.* *(Kenneth Gustafson)*

ment and workers are transported regularly to the site by the D&SNG. The electricity generated serves Durango, Purgatory ski area, and Silverton.

A spur track to the power plant was washed out in the flood of October 5, 1911, when heavy rains widened the river channel at Tacoma from 90 ft to 170 ft. Twenty-two miles of track were destroyed (photos, pp. 39, 137, 138). Retaining walls were built after another flood in September 1970.

During the spring, when the Animas River is high, rafters and kayakers who test their skills on an exciting ride down the river catch the eastbound train for Durango at Tacoma. Attempting a ride farther south through the Animas Canyon Gorge is foolhardy, to say the least.

Milepost
473   METAMORPHIC ROCK ALONG TRACK.
   For the next mile are outcrops of dark gray, layered gneiss with intruded masses of igneous diabase, gray granite, and some white quartz veins (pCsg). Diabase is a fine-grained, dark-gray-to-black igneous rock composed of plagio- clase feldspar and pyroxene. It often is used for tombstones.

Milepost
474   CABINS OF FORMER GUEST RANCH.
   Elev. 7,473 ft (2,278 m)
For 33 years (1952-1985) this was a well-known resort, Ah! Wilderness Guest Ranch. The only access to the guest ranch was by rail, foot, or horse- back. The buildings are used now to house the staff for Tall Timber Resort, located at mile 475.25. A five-car spur track on the east is used to store freight for Tall Timber Resort.

The buildings stand in a fairly flat valley, or park. The Animas Glacier gouged out a narrow trough which later was filled partly with stream allu- vium, a general term for unconsolidated materials deposited during Qua- ternary or recent time. In the fall, when the level of the river is low, round depressions or potholes in the rocks of the stream channel are visible. These potholes gradually were formed by water whirling stones and gravel around in one spot.

Wildflowers grow abundantly in this open park. Only a few scrub oak grow at this elevation, but aspen trees are becoming common. The aspen has a gray-green to white bark and round green leaves that are nearly al- ways moving, which gives it the name "quaking aspen" or "quakie." These slender, graceful trees often grow to 80 ft tall and may have trunks 10 to 12 inches in diameter.

From the east side of the train, look northwestward to the cliffs above the valley. If you are lucky, you may catch a quick glimpse of SILVER FALLS shimmering in the sun as the water tumbles down a cliff of the Ignacio Quartzite (Map No. 4). The trees have grown so much in the past 30 years the falls are difficult to see.

The October 5, 1911, Animas River flood washed out a spur track and bridge to the power plant at Tacoma. At the height of the flood, the river channel increased from 90 to 170 feet wide. *(Colorado Historical Society)*

The destructive force of water in the 1911 flood is well-illustrated in this photograph of a rail that was driven through a firm river willow stump. Twenty-two miles of track were washed away. Additional details of this flood are on p. 136. *(Colorado Historical Society)*

474.6 TANK CREEK WATER TANK.
Elev. 7,462 ft (2,274 m)

Westbound trains stop here to take water stored in a steel tank car body mounted on concrete supports. While just as efficient as the original wooden water tank, it is hardly as attractive. The original tank was removed in November 1966.

During this and at other stops, you may notice the crew getting off the train. Each member has important duties to perform while the train is stopped. The rear brakeman will walk down the track beyond the end of the train carrying a red box. He has been instructed by the engineer's whistle to "protect the rear of the train." By rule, the rear brakeman must take his "flagging kit" (a box containing red flags, flares, and railroad torpedoes) a prescribed distance down the track to warn any oncoming trains or railroad "speeders" that a train is stopped ahead. The head brakeman and conductor will use the opportunity to perform a brief visual inspection of the brake rigging and wheel assemblies under the coaches. The conductor may also meet with the engine crew, because this is the crew's only time to communicate other than by whistle and hand signals. Listen for the engineer to "call in the flag" just before the train is ready to move. Refer to the whistle guide on the inside front cover for this signal.

The track crosses Tank Creek, a roaring mountain stream that originates on the southern slope of Mountain View Crest, just before it enters the river at the water tank. This train stop affords a good opportunity to see how the river has cut through the gneiss and schist along joints and fractures. Lateral moraines are on both sides of the Animas in this portion of the canyon.

Water birch is common along the river and at the mouth of Tank Creek. This slender-stemmed tree with a shiny, dark bronze-to-copper bark grows to about 25 ft tall.

475.25 TALL TIMBER RESORT.

The small depot is a reception building for guests arriving or departing at this luxury, five-star, secluded resort. The only other access to Tall Timber is by helicopter. This open valley with lush aspen groves is a prime location for wildflowers. The Colorado state flower, the blue columbine, thrives in moist, shady aspen groves (photo, p. 55). It is found at elevations between 6,000 ft (1,800 m) and 11,000 ft (3,300 m) and blooms from late June in the lower elevations till mid-August higher in the mountains.

Although the track is on Quaternary alluvium deposits, Precambrian gabbro (pCgb) crops out on both sides of the valley between milepost 475 and mile 475.6. Gabbro is a dark-colored, equigranular igneous rock that

On July 17, 1951, an intentional head-on collision of D&RGW engines 319 and 345 was filmed on the Silverton Branch for the movie, "Denver and Rio Grande." The scene was set in the open park at milepost 475, at what is now Tall Timber Resort. Engine 345, on the right, was renumbered 268 for the movie. Both engines were ruined in the collision and were dismantled in the fall of 1951.   *(Center for Southwest Studies, Ft. Lewis College)*

was injected as a hot fluid into the older gneisses and schists, probably about 2 billion years ago. Boundaries between the different types of igneous rocks commonly are irregular and indefinite.

Several movies were filmed in this small park. A replica of an 1880 town was built here for the movie, "Denver and Rio Grande." The climax of this epic was the intentional head-on collision and destruction of two of the railroad's locomotives. At the time (1951), the D&RGW management viewed the narrow gauge as an obsolete misfit suitable only for junking.

Parts of "Night Passage," "Ticket to Tomahawk" (photo, p. 67), "Naked Spur," and "Around the World in 80 Days" also were filmed along the Silverton Branch. A number of other movies have been filmed at other sites in the San Juans, including "Colorado Territory," "Across the Wide Missouri," "Viva Zapata," "Three Young Texans," "Run for Cover," "Maverick Queen," "How the West was Won," "Butch Cassidy and the Sundance Kid," "Support your Local Gunfighter," and "The Tracker." During the fall of 1994, a sequel to the Ken Burns' production on the Civil War, entitled "The West," was filmed on the Silverton Branch.

476.1 Cross Grasshopper Creek.

The bridge was completely refurbished during the winter of 1993-94. Cement trucks were hauled to the site on flatcars to pour the footings.

This stream begins on Mountain View Crest (Map No. 5, p. 44). An alluvial fan is at the mouth of the creek.

Blue spruce, Colorado's state tree, is becoming more numerous with the higher elevation. It is a beautiful, tapered tree that sometimes reaches 120 ft in height. The needles are sharp, stiff, a silvery gray-green color and ½-1¼ inches long and curved. The cones are 2½-4 inches long. The bark is a dark gray.

Colorado blue spruce

476.7 Little Cascade Creek.

This stream joins the Animas River on the west. A concrete retaining wall was built after the 1970 flood.

477 Enter Small Open Park.

Small rock slides are along the east side of the valley. Columbines are abundant here in July.

477.5 Cascade Canyon Wye.
Elev. 7,696 ft (2,346 m)

This wye, built in 1981, is used to turn the **Cascade Canyon Winter Train** that makes a delightful, 52-mile round trip from Durango.

During the summer, a red boxcar often will be parked at the tail of the wye. The boxcar may look like an ordinary piece of railroad equipment, but on the inside it is a modern RV camper for families or small groups who wish to spend a week fishing, hiking or train-watching.

Cascade Canyon enters the Animas River from the northwest, a short distance north of the wye. This narrow canyon opens up into a small park-like area called Purgatory Flats which is about three miles northwest of the mouth of Cascade Creek. In this flat, Purgatory Creek and Lime Creek join Cascade Creek. How the name "Purgatory" evolved is not known, but one version suggests that the narrow, steep-walled section of Cascade Creek is called Purgatory because it is hard to get in and hard to get out!

The winter of 1878-79 was one of the mildest on record all over the West. In April 1979, fires started at a number of places in the mountains to the west and northwest, and did not burn themselves out until the following September. By June, Cascade Creek Canyon and Purgatory Flats were at the center of an ever-expanding wall of flames. Throughout the summer, fires raged along Lime Creek, extending as far north as the Molas Mine, located on the hill above mile 493.3. More than 26,000 acres of timber were burned, much of it on the east side of U.S. 550. Silverton escaped, but suffocating smoke filled Baker's Park for many weeks.

Mile
477.75   TEFFT FLAG STOP.
The original location of Tefft Station was at 477.9. The D&SNG moved the stop to this point to allow easier loading and unloading of passengers and freight.

Mile
477.8   CROSSES ANIMAS RIVER.
The north span of this wrought-iron bridge was built in 1887 and placed here in 1911. The south steel span was built in 1972. The Needle Mountains are on the skyline to the northeast.

Mile
477.9   ORIGINAL LOCATION OF TEFFT.
Elev. 7,712 ft (2,351 m)
This station is named for Guy Tefft, an early-day forest ranger. It is also the location of Niccora, a short-lived way station on the toll road started by Frank E. Blackledge, who also petitioned for a post office. The post office operated from July 16, 1877, to November 26, 1877, when Blackledge, the postmaster, left for the winter and never returned. During 1878, Thomas Charlton briefly considered building a hotel at the site of Blackledge's cabins. A cabin standing on the north side of Cascade Creek is probably on the site of Niccora. This cabin, built in 1941, is owned by Ernie Schaaf of Durango.

A large sawmill, built in the 1890s and operated by the Matevie brothers, was located here. It produced mine timbers and railroad ties for the D&RG and the Silverton Northern RR. Timber was cut from spruce-fir forests along Cascade and Lime Creeks and floated to the mill. Remains of the locomotive boiler from the Silverton Northern engine *Gold King* are hidden almost completely from view on the hillside northwest of this point.

The Animas Canyon Toll Road from Silverton to Animas City was along the west side of the Animas River to Tefft. The grade is now very difficult to find and, in many places, the railroad was built on the old road. At Tefft, the road crossed Cascade Creek and climbed the rather open Cascade Hill to the west in a series of three switchbacks. It took six horses to pull the stages to the top of Cascade Hill where another way station, operated by homesteader Sam Smith, was located. From the top, the toll road

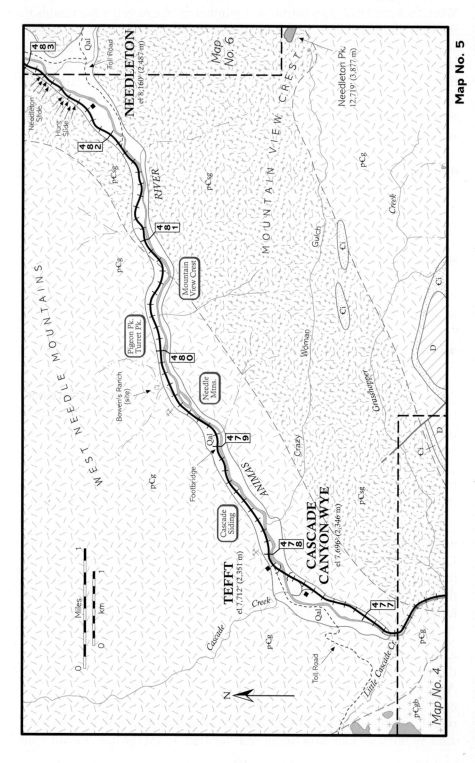

NEEDLETON
el 8,160' (2,487 m)

Map
No. 6

MOUNTAIN VIEW CREST

Needleton Pk.
12,719' (3,877 m)

Qal

Toll Road

Needleton
Slide

Hunt
Slide

4 8 3

4 8 2

pCsg

RIVER

pCsg

pCg

4 8 1

Mountain
View Crest

Gulch

Creek

pCg

Ci

Ci

Pigeon Pk.
Turret Pk.

4 8 0

Ci

Woman

Ci

Needle
Mtns.

Bower's Ranch
(site)

W E S T   N E E D L E   M O U N T A I N S

Grasshopper

D

4 7 9

Qal

Crazy

D

Footbridge

pCg

ANIMAS

pCsg

Ci

Cascade
Siding

CASCADE
CANYON WYE
el 7,696' (2,346 m)

4 7 8

TEFFT
el 7,712' (2,351 m)

Cascade

Creek

4 7 7

Miles
1

0

km
1

Qal

pCg

pCg

Toll Road

0

N

Little Cascade Cr.

pCgb

44

crossed Little Cascade Creek and continued south along Elbert Creek, passing Rockwood, Pinkerton's ranch, and Hermosa, following in a general way the present route of U.S. 550 highway. There were toll gates at Baker's Bridge, (Map No. 3, p. 27) and in the canyon below Silverton. The fare was $6 one way, which was very expensive at that time Additional details on the toll road are on p. 76.

Milepost
478 SILVER STAR MINE.

Some lead, zinc, and silver were produced from this mine on the west side of the track. Four claims were staked along here in 1910 by Frederick Schaaf. These claims were leased by Oscar J. Grace of Oklahoma City in 1941, and a short time later they were taken over by Oscar Schaaf, who subsequently passed the claims on to his nephew, Ernie Schaaf. The Silver Star is the only remaining claim which still is owned by Ernie Schaaf.

Mile
478.4 CASCADE SIDING SIGN.
Elev. 7,785 ft (2,373 m)

At one time a siding, stock pen, section house, bunkhouse, and coal house were on the west side of the track. The railroad was completed to this point on June 7, 1882.

Milepost
479 VALLEY NARROWS.

A footbridge crosses the Animas. It is used by U.S. Forest Service personnel, fishermen and backpackers. The cabin across the river belongs to Ross McCausland, who built and operated the Ah! Wilderness Guest Ranch.

Mile
479.5 BITTER ROOT MINE.

The remains of this mining venture are on the left side of the track. Oscar Schaaf and his wife came to the Animas Canyon in the 1930s and took over some placer claims that had been staked by a man named Brown. The mine was named by Oscar's wife for her former home in the Bitterroot Mountains of Montana.

Mile
479.6 NEEDLE MOUNTAINS SIGN.

Throughout this section of the canyon are dramatic vistas of the sharp, jagged peaks to the northeast. Pigeon Peak, elevation 13,961 ft (4,255 m), is on the left; Turret Peak, elevation 13,619 ft (4,151 m) is on the right.

Trees are mostly tall aspens, some subalpine firs, willows, spruce, ponderosa pines, limber pines, lodgepole pines, and Douglas firs. Douglas fir has a gray-to-reddish-brown bark that is thick and deeply furrowed. This straight-trunked tree grows to 100 ft tall; the upper branches point up while the lower ones droop and re-curve. The needles are a bright green color, ³/₄-1 inch long and flattened. The cones are 1¹/₄-2 inches long and hang down with three-pointed bracts sticking out between the cone scales

Subalpine fir is a 60-90 ft tall, spire-like tree. The bark is thin, hard, ash-gray-to-whitish color. The lower branches are long and droopy. The needles are a blue-green color, 1-1³/₄ inches long, flattened and curved upward. The purplish-brown cones are 3-4 inches long and stand upright on the branches.

Douglas fir   Subalpine fir

Mile
479.7   SITE OF BOWEN'S RANCH.

In 1878, William C. Bowen and his wife, Jane, moved from Silverton and established a small ranch and way station for travelers on the toll road. The circumstances under which the couple left Silverton are clouded, but the Bowens had owned a grocery store, the Westminster Hall (saloon and bordello). Jane was known as "Aunt Jane" or "Sage Hen" while running her business in Silverton. The D&RG purchased a right-of-way through the Bowen property in 1880, and the Bowens returned to Silverton to run their businesses.

Oscar Schaaf and his wife lived in the Animas Canyon for many years. He built a small mill and concentrating table to process the small amount of ore he found in his claims. He moved two buildings from Cascade Siding to this site. Oscar Schaaf was the official fire warden for many years, and was well known for his mechanical abilities—including a motorized track car he built, the remains of which are still at Tefft. Oscar Schaaf deeded his property to another nephew, Mel Schaaf, who died in the early 1980s.

Lodgepole pines are tall, slender conifers up to 100 ft tall with paired yellow-green needles from 1¹/₂-3 inches long. The cones remain on the trees for years without opening to drop their seed.

Lodgepole pine

46

480.1   PIGEON PEAK—TURRET PEAK SIGN.

There are many chances for excellent photos of these peaks and of your train as it winds through the 20° curves along the Animas River.

480.5   MOUNTAIN VIEW CREST SIGN.

To the southeast, it is easy to see how this range acted as a barrier to the ice moving down the Animas canyon (p. 16). Glacially rounded gravel and boulders are strewn along the river. A waterfall is across the river.

A long-abandoned mine, known as "Pajarito" (Little Parrot) was west of the track.

480.7   CONTACT OF GRANITE AND METAMORPHIC ROCKS.

Light gray Twilight Granite (p€g) was emplaced about 1.5 billion years ago. The banded, angular, blocky outcrops of older metamorphic gneiss and schist (p€sg) are markedly different from the rounded, smoothed, and glacially polished granite. Note the large size of the aspen trees.

481.5   LOWER END OF NEEDLETON PARK.

Upstream is an excellent view of Pigeon Peak. Portions of the San Juan Mountains, including the Needle Mountains, were designated as the San Juan Wilderness in 1965. In 1975, the area was enlarged to become the Weminuche Wilderness, the largest in the contiguous 48 states. It encompasses some 460,000 acres and extends eastward along the Continental Divide to Wolf Creek Pass. Four peaks, Mount Eolus, North Eolus, Sunlight Peak, and Windom Peak, are over 14,000 ft (4,270 m) and are popular destinations for mountain climbers (photo, p. 52).

482.31   ORIGINAL SITE OF NEEDLETON.
    Elev. 8,160 ft (2,487 m)

The original Needleton station was washed away in the 1927 flood.

This was a stop on the stage road and the departure point for optimistic prospectors who flocked to Chicago Basin in the Needle Mountains in the 1880s. Interest in the area increased after the D&RG track reached Needleton June 14, 1882. Remarkably, a post office was established in May 1882 and lasted until January 10, 1919. The first postmaster was Theodore Schock, who had a post office at the top of Cascade Hill along the toll road but moved to Needleton when the Silverton Branch was completed. Additional history of the area begins on pp. 80-81.

47

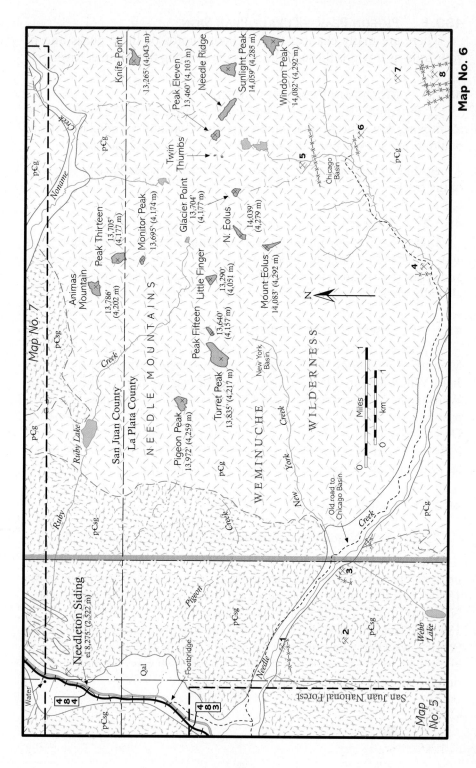

Knife Point
13,265' (4,043 m)

Peak Eleven
13,460' (4,103 m)

Needle Ridge

Sunlight Peak
14,059' (4,285 m)

Windom Peak
14,082' (4,292 m)

Twin Thumbs

Peak Thirteen
13,705'
(4,177 m)

Monitor Peak
13,695' (4,174 m)

Glacier Point
13,704'
(4,177 m)

N. Eolus
14,039'
(4,279 m)

Animas Mountain
13,786'
(4,202 m)

Little Finger
13,290'
(4,051 m)

Mount Eolus
14,083' (4,292 m)

Peak Fifteen
13,640'
(4,157 m)

Turret Peak
13,835' (4,217 m)

Pigeon Peak
13,972' (4,259 m)

N

New York Basin

N E E D L E   M O U N T A I N S

W E M I N U C H E

W I L D E R N E S S

Chicago Basin

Old road to Chicago Basin

San Juan County
La Plata County

Ruby Lake

Noname Creek

Ruby

Creek

Creek

New York Creek

New Creek

Creek

pꞒg

pꞒsg

pꞒg

pꞒg

pꞒsg

pꞒg

pꞒsg

pꞒsg

Map No. 7

Miles
0   1
km
0   1

Needleton Siding
el 8,275' (2,522 m)

Qal

Footbridge

Pigeon

Needle

Creek

San Juan National Forest

Webb Lake

Water

4 8 4

4 8 3

Map No. 5

48

Mile
482.5   HUNT SLIDE.

This slide, named for A.C. Hunt, an early-day D&RG official, traverses the steep western slope when snowfall is unusually heavy. The area also is subject to mudslides during heavy rains. In January 1997 mud and debris from this slide were removed and the grade was realigned to eliminate a sharp curve.

Mile
482.8   NEEDLETON SNOWSLIDE.

This slide also comes down the steep western slope and often covers the track. From here to Silverton are numerous steep, almost vertical channel-like gullies that are pathways for huge snowslides (avalanches) that roar down the slopes after heavy winter storms. Vegetation is unable to grow to any height in these paths. Trees, shrubs, rocks, and snow all end up on the track or in the river as huge mounds, sometimes from to 40-80 ft deep.

Mile
482.85   NEEDLE CREEK CANYON SIGN.

This sign is just above the Needleton snowslide. Needle Creek joins the Animas River from the east, flowing across an alluvial fan. The trail to Chicago Basin follows Needle Creek.

Look eastward up Needle Creek to the incredibly beautiful, horn-shaped peaks of the Needle Mountains that stand 500-1,000 ft (150-300 m) above the glaciers that filled the valleys. It is easy to see why the San Juans are called the "Alps of America."

Milepost
483   MILEPOST AT EDGE OF OPEN MEADOW.

Many wildflowers, grasses, and ferns grow in this meadow. In the early summer, Rocky Mountain iris grows in these moist open meadows. The flowers are a variegated violet-blue color, about 2-3 inches long and on stalks 1-2 ft tall. The rootstocks of this plant have a strong, disagreeable odor and contain the poison, irisin, a violent emetic and cathartic. Yarrow (milfoil or tansy) is another interesting flower that grows throughout the mountains from the lowest valleys to timberline. This flat-topped plant with many small white flowers in small heads or clusters grows to a height of 1 to 3 ft. The Indians used yarrow for a stimulant and tonic.

Mile
483.3   NEEDLETON FLAG STOP.

There is a footbridge here and trains stop to let off hikers, backpackers, and rafters going down the river. Most backpackers head for Chicago Ba-

49

Newly-restored engine 497 steams past the Needleton water tank in July 1984.

A Durango-bound D&SNG train, powered by engine 478, winds along the tumbling Animas River between Tall Timber and Tank Creek.

(Both photos, Kenneth T. Gustafson)

sin and the high peaks of the Needle Mountains in the Weminuche Wilderness. Buildings across the river are privately owned. On the southern skyline is a good view of Mountain View Crest.

Mile
483.7   LA PLATA-SAN JUAN COUNTY LINE.
A sharp curve here is known as Dieckman's Curve, in honor of John Dieckman, D&RGW engineer who ran engine 473 into the river at this point because of a kink in the track caused by heat expansion (photo, p. 149).

Milepost
484   NEEDLETON SIDING SIGN.
Elev. 8,293 ft (2,528 m)
This 525-ft siding was placed here after the 1927 flood, when the river moved into a new channel between mile 481.8 and milepost 483. Aspens, birches, river willows, and subalpine firs, in addition to raspberries and countless wildflowers, thrive in this park.

Mile
484.2   SOLID BOWMAN MINE.
This prospect, on the east side of the river, was reported to have had some gold-bearing pyrite veins.

Mile
484.4   NEEDLETON TANK.
It takes lots of water to make the steam which propels your train up the 2.5% grade, so water tanks must to be placed at strategic locations to quench the engine's thirst. A stop for water is made on both the up and down trips (photos, pp. 50 and 52). The wooden water tank was retired in the 1960s, and a tank car body, located about 200 ft north of the old tank, now serves the same purpose. Water comes from a small reservoir on the hill. The Needleton tank and the tank at Hermosa are the last wooden tanks on the Silverton Branch.

The toll road is visible through the trees on the west slope. To the east is a good view of Pigeon Peak.

The west side of the Animas Canyon forms the base of the Twilight Peaks that are two miles to the west and stand one mile above the bottom of the canyon. These peaks are not visible from the train.

Mile
484.5   MOUNT GARFIELD AND GRAYSTONE PEAK.
These two spectacular 13,000-ft peaks (3,960 m) are visible up the valley to the northeast. Both are in the Grenadier Range (Map No. 7, p. 54).

Mile
484.6   RUBY CREEK SIGN.
This creek plunges into the Animas River from the east. Several avalanche tracks and rock glaciers are along the west side of the track.

Geologist Whitman Cross took this spectacular photo July 12, 1901, from the summit of Mountain View Crest looking northward across Needle Creek Canyon to the beautiful faceted horns of Pigeon Peak, Turret Peak, and Mt. Eolus, from left to right.

(U.S. Geological Survey)

Northbound freight taking water at Needleton tank, mile 484.4, probably during the 1940s.

(Colorado Historical Society)

Trees include alpine fir, willow, aspen, Englemann spruce, and limber pine. The Englemann spruce is a compact tree up to 125 ft tall with a smooth, cinnamon-brown trunk. The needles are dark blue-green, about 1 inch long. The cones are 1-3 inches long.

Englemann spruce

Limber pine is named for its flexible branches with needles 1¼-3 inches long that are crowded in bundles of five at the ends of twigs. This conifer is up to 80 ft tall. From here to Silverton, the assemblage of plants and animals is typical of the Montane Life Zone.

Limber pine

Milepost
485   GRANITE CLIFFS.
For the next four miles the track is built on Precambrian Twilight Granite, named for the Twilight peaks in the West Needle Mountains. Notice how the light gray granite cliffs on both sides of the track have been rounded, smoothed, and polished by the Animas glacier.

Mile
485.4   NO NAME SNOWSLIDE.
This snowslide descends the steep western valley opposite the point where Noname Creek cascades across a moraine to join the Animas River.

A short distance north of this slide, at mile 485.5, are Noname Rapids which present a real challenge for rafters and kayakers who make their way down the river from May until mid-July. Watch for big, smooth rocks in the river at this narrow bottleneck.

Mile
485.7   MOUNTAIN VIEW CREST SIGN.
There is a good view to the south of this range. When the water level is low, potholes in the river channel are visible.

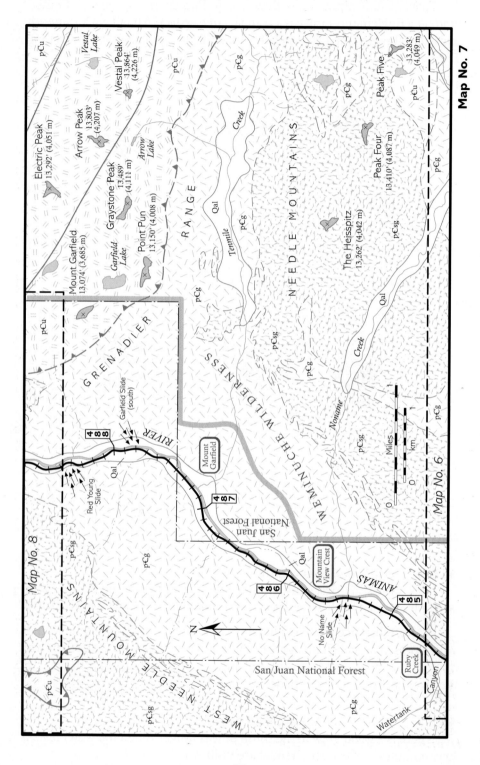

Electric Peak
13,292' (4,051 m)

Vestal
Lake

Vestal Peak
13,864'
(4,226 m)

Arrow Peak
13,803'
(4,207 m)

Mount Garfield
13,074' (3,685 m)

Graystone Peak
13,489'
(4,111 m)

Garfield
Lake

Point Pun
13,150' (4,008 m)

Arrow
Lake

pCu

pCu

pCu

pCg

Creek

pCg

pCg

Peak Five
13,283'
(4,049 m)

Peak Four
13,410' (4,087 m)

The Heisspitz
13,262' (4,042 m)

pCu

pCsg

pCg

pCg

Qal

pCg

Tenmile

RANGE

NEEDLE MOUNTAINS

pCg

pCsg

pCg

pCsg

Noname

Creek

Qal

GRENADIER

WEMINUCHE WILDERNESS

Garfield Slide
(south)

488

RIVER

Qal

Red Young
Slide

pCsg

Mount
Garfield

487

San Juan
National Forest

pCg

486

Qal

Mountain
View Crest

485

No Name
Slide

ANIMAS

Ruby
Creek

Canyon

Watertank

N

San Juan National Forest

WEST NEEDLE MOUNTAINS

pCu

pCsg

pCg

pCu

Miles

km

1

1

0

0

Map No. 8

Map No. 6

Rocky mountain splendor in the Animas canyon. This lovely view, just south of milepost 486, looks northeast toward Mount Garfield in the Grenadier Range. The columbines growing beside the track are Colorado's state flower. *(Richard L. Hunter)*

486   High Peaks of the Grenadier Range.

Glimpses of these beautiful peaks are visible to the northeast. Granite outcrops have been rounded and polished by the Animas Glacier moving slowly southward.

Mile
486.5   Site of Mudslides.

During the spring runoff and heavy rains during the summer, mudslides are a constant problem and often cover the track.

Milepost
487   Steepest Grade on Silverton Branch.

Even though the track profile states the ruling grade is a constant 2.5%, for the next mile the actual grade is 3% with short sections of nearly 4% at milepost 488. Now the fireman is shoveling coal at a furious pace to keep the engine at full throttle.

Mile
487.15   Tenmile Creek Tumbles into the Animas.
Elev. 8,641 ft (2,634 m)

It is believed that the toll road builders named this stream that is exactly 10 miles from Silverton. In 1880, Franz Armine Schneider and his family moved to this open level area along Tenmile Creek and started an establishment known as Ten Mile House. Horses could be changed, and as Allen Nossaman so aptly described conditions of travel on the toll road, Tenmile Creek was "frequently the transition point from moderate to miserable weather for northbound travel during the winter in the canyon." The old toll road still is visible in the trees above the track. Schneider kept a team of dogs which often were called upon to carry mail, supplies, and even drinking water to Silverton on sleds when the track was blocked beyond his place.

The mountain to the southeast is the westernmost extension of a ridge west of Monitor Peak in the Needle Mountains (Map No. 6). Other high peaks are located on the map.

Mile
487.25   Mount Garfield Sign.

This sign is visible on the westbound trip.

Mile
487.9   Garfield Snowslide.

Most winters this slide (photo, p. 57) crosses the river and plows into the track. Two large slides come down the steep slopes of Mount Garfield; the northern slide is at mile 489.5. From here to milepost 495, the train crosses the paths of many snowslides, making this the most difficult section of track to open. Every spring, locomotives equipped with pilot plows

The southern snowslide off Mount Garfield at mile 487.8, as it looked June 4, 1965.
(F.W. Osterwald)

This magnificent view of Electric, Arrow, and Vestal Peaks, from right to left, was taken in August 1903 by geologist Ernest Howe. He was standing across Elk Creek on a high ridge looking south-southwest. *(U.S. Geological Survey)*

pull flatcars loaded with bulldozers to this area. The bulldozers then go to work clearing the track (photo, p. 158). Because so much debris is carried in the snow, rotary plows never were used.

During the 1980s, the D&SNG realigned the track through this section to reduce the curves and ease the hard pull for longer trains.

Milepost
488   PLACER MINING OPERATION.

Remnants of a placer mining operation are across the river. The operation was not successful because the sand, rocks, and boulders of many sizes are mixed together in a a jumbled manner, making it difficult to separate and find flakes of gold.

Mile
488.5   RED YOUNG SLIDE.

This slide, on the west side of the track, was named for an early-day engineer, William (Red) Young, who was killed when his engine slammed into a snowslide in 1897. His is one of the few railroad fatalities that resulted from a snowslide. Sometimes, when the slides were particularly deep, it was easier to tunnel through than to remove all the snow from the track. Additional details on snow problems are on pp. 132-136, 158.

Milepost
489   UNNAMED STREAM JOINS ANIMAS.

This steep mountain stream on the west has its source on the southern slope of Snowden Peak, named in honor of Francis M. Snowden, a miner who built the first cabin in Silverton in 1874.

In this area, the Animas Canyon is about 4,200 ft deep, and a little less than three miles wide.

The boundary between Precambrian granite and Precambrian metamorphic rocks is very irregular and indistinct. The layered outcrops of gneiss and schist stand vertical in blocky cliffs. Granite outcrops are smoother and more rounded.

Mile
489.5   CROSS MAJOR FAULT ZONE.

Map No. 8 (p. 59) shows a major thrust fault that crosses the Animas Valley at this point. Precambrian Uncompahgre Quartzite (p€u) is faulted against Precambrian gneisses and schists (p€sg). Note the tight folds in the shiny, gray quartzite which was deposited as sand by rivers flowing into a sea about 1 billion years ago. Between here and milepost 492 are several more east-west trending faults.

The northern Garfield Slide comes down the north slope of the peak through a narrow, V-shaped fault valley. Snow may remain piled in the stream until mid-June.

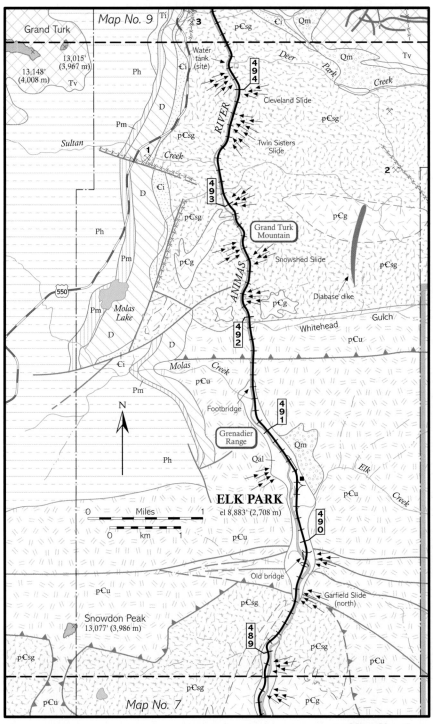

Grand Turk

13,015'
(3,967 m)
13,148'
(4,008 m)
Tv

Ti

3

pCsg   Ci   Qm

Ph

Ci   Water
      tank
      (site)

Deer   Qm   Tv

Park

Creek

D

RIVER

**4
9
4**

Cleveland Slide

pCsg

Pm

Sultan

pCsg

Creek

Twin Sisters
Slide

1

D   Ci

pCsg

**4
9
3**

pCg

Grand Turk
Mountain

pCg

2

Ph

Pm

pCg

ANIMAS

Snowshed Slide

pCg

Diabase dike

pCsg

550

Pm   Molas
      Lake

D

D

Ci

Pm

**4
9
2**

Whitehead   Gulch

pCu

Molas   Creek

pCu

N

Footbridge

**4
9
1**

Grenadier
Range

Qm

Ph

Qal

pCu

Elk

Creek

ELK PARK
el 8,883' (2,708 m)

0   Miles   1

0   km   1

**4
9
0**

pCu

pCu

Old bridge

Garfield Slide
(north)

pCu   pCsg

Snowdon Peak
13,077' (3,986 m)

pCsg

**4
8
9**

pCsg

pCu

pCsg

pCu

pCu

pCsg   pCg

59

On August 11, 1903, Ernest Howe captured this afternoon scene along the Animas River about a mile above Elk Park. Mount Garfield dominates the skyline, while Electric Peak is on the far left, and Graystone Peak is in between. These peaks are part of the Grenadier Range.

(U.S. Geological Survey)

489.85 CROSS ANIMAS RIVER.
This two-span, 222-ft steel deck plate girder bridge was installed in 1964. The track makes a wide curve here before entering the main part of Elk Park. The best view of the old four-span through truss timber bridge built in 1884 is visible to the west while crossing the "new" bridge. The old bridge was abandoned in 1964 because the abutments were weakened by spring runoffs.

Mile
490.15 MINCO SPUR.
A two-car spur occasionally is used by a small uranium mining operation uphill to the west.

Mile
490.3 CROSS ELK CREEK.
To the west, across the river, folds in the metamorphic Uncompahgre Quartzite (p€u) are clearly visible.

Mile
490.5 ELK PARK.
Elev. 8,883 ft (2,707 m)

A siding and wye are located at this site. At one time there was also a section house, bunkhouse and a coal bin. This station is also a flag stop for fishermen and for backpackers who use the steep trail along Elk Creek into the Needle Mountains. The Colorado Trail follows Elk Creek eastward.

The frantic pace of laying hand-hewn ties on the roadbed and spiking down 30-lb steel rail continued without interruption throughout the spring of 1882, and by June 27, 1882, construction trains were running to Elk Park. In 1884, a wye was built so trains could be turned when the track between Silverton and Elk Park was blocked by snowslides. A stub turnout, with a harp-type switch stand, was installed. This unusual switch stand, the last one in use in Colorado, was removed by 1973. At one time there were stock pens for loading and unloading sheep.

This open, grassy park is filled with wildflowers. In the spring, white candytuft is common, along with dandelions. Dandelions, which are socially unacceptable in city lawns, are beautiful in the mountains in early June. The flowers and leaves are a favorite food of grouse, elk, deer, bear, and porcupine. The roots have been used for centuries for tonics, diuretics, and mild laxatives. The leaves are used in salads and the blossoms for making wine. Summer brings the columbines, mountain parsley, ferns, Indian paintbrushes, shrub cinquefoil, penstemons, lupines, primroses, and gentians. In September, yarrow, goldenrod, fall asters, and daisies are abundant.

Some avalanche tracks are directly across the river. A large moraine (Qm on Map No. 8, p. 59) is along the east side of the valley. The river has reworked and shifted the morainal deposits and combined them with stream gravel.

Mile
491.2   GRENADIER RANGE SIGN.

This sign is visible on the return trip. Look southward down the valley for glimpses of Graystone and Electric Peaks, along with a very good view of Mount Garfield. To the south, momentary glimpses of Arrow and Vestal Peaks may be seen before the train leaves Elk Park. Map No. 7 (p. 54) shows the location of these high peaks of the Grenadier Range that stood above the surrounding ice fields.

Mile
491.3   MOLAS CREEK.

This stream, which heads on Molas Pass, joins the Animas here. A footbridge across the Animas River is used by hikers following the famous Colorado Trail that starts near Denver and ends in Durango, passing through some 475 miles of high mountain passes and incredible beauty.

The rocks in the river channel are stained a reddish-brown due to chemicals in the water which have been leached from the mill tailing ponds that operated near Silverton at one time (photo, p. 63).

Mile
491.65   TRACK CROSSES LARGE EAST-WEST THRUST FAULT.

Mile
491.95   WHITEHEAD GULCH.
Elev. 8,981 ft (2,737 m)

Sometime after the Silverton water tank at mile 494.2 was removed in 1924, a water spout was rigged at the mouth of this steep gulch to deliver water to thirsty engines. The spout was used until the 1950s, or perhaps early 1960s. The spout and flume were washed out before, or possibly during, the 1970 flood.

Between Whitehead Gulch and the Snowshed Slide at mile 492.5 is the final steep grade before reaching Silverton.

The old toll road is visible on the hillside to the west, across the river. Old rails lying in the Animas are stark reminders of past floods.

Whitehead Gulch follows an east-west fault that is easily seen looking west across the river. The fault brings the Uncompahgre Quartzite in contact with gneiss and schist. There are also two small, irregular masses of reddish-pink granite that crop out on each side of the river. (Map No. 8, p. 59).

View northward below milepost 495. This dramatic photo, taken in the fall when the water level is low, reveals how iron-rich minerals from mine dumps and mine drainages have been carried into the Animas River and deposited on the rocks as rusty, yellow-brown iron oxide stains. *(Anthony Frank)*

Names of old mines shown on Map No. 9:
1. Champion Mine
2. Detroit Mine
3. King Mine
4. Belcher (Sultan Mtn.)
5. Montezuma Mine
6. Empire Tunnel
7. North Star (Sultan Mtn.)
8. Marcella Mine
9. Idaho Mine
10. Mighty Monarch
11. Scranton City Mine
12. Blair Mountain Mine
13. Little Giant Mine
14. Amy Tunnel
15. Legal Tender Tunnel
16. Aspen Group
17. Happy Jack
18. Black Prince Mine
19. Shenandoah-Dives Mine
20. Unity Mine
21. Nevada Mine
22. New York Mine
23. Silver Lake Mine
24. Iowa Mine
25. Royal Tiger Mine
26. Titusville Mine
27. Buckeye Mine

Following the removal of the water tank that once stood at mile 494.2, D&RGW officials took this photo in May 1924 showing the wooden platform remaining at the site. *(Album of Water Rights, Center for Southwest Studies, Ft. Lewis College)*

This gulch is near the southern margin of the highly mineralized area along the southern flank of the Silverton caldera. Veins in this area are numerous, but usually short and narrow, and ore minerals are irregularly distributed in them.

Mile
492.5 SNOWSHED SLIDE.

The timber side sills and concrete walls are all that remain of a 339-ft long snow shed built in 1890 to protect the track from two slides that converged at this point. The shed was burned July 23, 1917, and was replaced by a 400-ft shed. The date this second shed was removed is not known. At one time there was a small shack where a caretaker lived during the snowshed days. The building was destroyed during a fire in 1981.

From here to milepost 495 are many snowslides, most of which have no name. They are either too small or do not commonly cover the track.

Mile
492.8 GRAND TURK MOUNTAIN SIGN.

Views of the majestic twin summits are visible to the northwest.

Mile
493.35 MOLAS MINE ON THE WEST.

Look up the steep valley of Sultan Creek for a glimpse of the Molas Mine, located about 1,200 ft above the Animas River. It produced ore from a mineralized fault.

From here to Silverton, hundreds of dangerous mine dumps, the remains of shacks, and collapsing mine buildings are visible on the steep hillsides offering stark evidence of Silverton's rich mining heritage. Maps 8 and 9 show the locations of many mines in the area and illustrate the complicated geology.

Mile
493.6 TWIN SISTERS SLIDE.

Milepost
494 CLEVELAND SLIDE.

Both slides run regularly each year.

The continental divide is parallel to the railroad, six miles to the east.

Mile
494.2 SITE OF WATER TANK.

The Silverton water tank was located on the east side of the track, a short distance south of the Deer Park Creek. The tank was removed in 1924 (photo, p. 63). The cement foundations still are visible along the east side of the track.

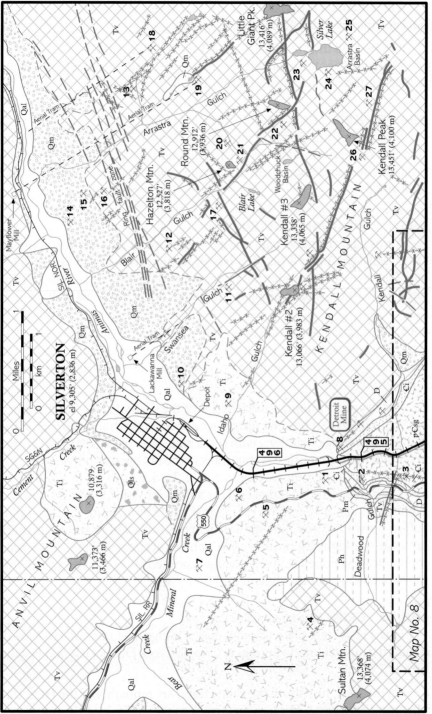

Map No. 9

SILVERTON
el 9,305' (2,836 m)

Little Giant Pk.
13,416'
(4,089 m)

Silver Lake

Arrastra Basin ×25

Round Mtn.
12,912'
(3,936 m)

Arrastra Gulch

Hazelton Mtn.
12,527'
(3,818 m)

Blair Lake

Kendall #3
13,338'
(4,065 m)

Kendall Peak
×13,451' (4,100 m)

Kendall #2
13,066' (3,983 m)

KENDALL MOUNTAIN

Kendall Gulch

Detroit Mine

Anvil Mountain

10,879'
(3,316 m)

11,373'
(3,466 m)

Sultan Mtn.
13,368'
(4,074 m)

Deadwood Gulch

Swansea

Lackawanna Mill

Depot

Idaho

Ring fault zone

Aerial Tram

Mayflower Mill

SIL. NOR.

Animas River

Cement Creek

Mineral Creek

Bear Creek

SIL. RR

550

N

Miles

km

Map No. 8

65

494.6   REMAINS OF ORE TIPPLE ON EAST.

The remains of an old boiler are also at this site. Across the river, the bucket cable from the King Mine is visible.

Just beyond the ore tipple, the track crosses Kendall Creek which heads on Kendall Mountain, named for James W. Kendall, one of the original owners of the famous North Star mine.

494.65   KING MINE.

Remains of this mine (number 3 on Map No. 9, p. 63) are on the hillside across the river in a steep gulch aptly named Cataract. An aerial tram brought silver and copper ore to a loading dock and spur track located at mile 494.8.

495   DEADWOOD GULCH.

Across the river and high on the steep slope of this gulch was the DE-TROIT MINE (number 2 on Map No. 9). It produced silver, zinc, and copper. The creek flows under the remains of the old mine building. A spur track to the tram station along the main track was removed in 1924.

495.25   CROSS ANIMAS RIVER.

This is the last crossing of the Animas before arriving in Silverton. The bridge is a deck timber structure that has been featured in countless railroad photographs.

Just beyond the bridge, the remains of the CHAMPION MINE (number 1 on Map No. 9) can be seen on the west side of the track. Copper sulfide and silver-bearing ores, along with some zinc, were produced from the mine in considerable quantities. A spur track to the ore bin was removed in 1924. The mine is located on the contact of a Tertiary quartz monzonite (Ti) mass that was intruded (emplaced) as a fluid into the Ouray and Leadville Limestones about 10 million years ago. Quartz monzonite is a light tan-to-buff-to-brown colored, fine-grained igneous rock. Other workings up the hill near the highway on this same contact account for the bright green copper-bearing minerals that are being deposited along the steep gulch from water that flows out the mine portal.

496.15   CROSS MINERAL CREEK.

This 112-ft steel plate through-girder bridge was built in 1907 for the standard gauge Colorado Springs & Cripple Creek District RR and installed here in 1916.

On the west, just above the valley floor, are remnants of the HERCULES MINE and MELVILLE MILL. A spur track to the mill joined the mainline at milepost 496.

496.3 SILVERTON WYE.

While you are visiting Silverton, your train will back down to this wye, where it will turn around and be brought back up to 12th and Blair Streets for re-boarding.

Silverton has the distinction of being the only town in the United States once served by four narrow gauge railroads. In addition to the former D&RG on which you are riding, the Silverton Railroad, the Silverton, Gladstone and Northerly, and the Silverton Northern traversed the alpine canyons to serve the mines to the north and northwest of Silverton (Map No. 9). Additional data concerning these railroads are on p. 85.

Mile
496.7 SILVERTON DEPOT.

In 1969, the D&RGW donated the depot to the San Juan Historical Society. The D&SNG purchased the building in 1985. An agent is on duty in the summer months to conduct the railroad's business. Other buildings that once stood near the depot included a section house, a bunkhouse, and a coal house. A new 20-car siding was installed in 1986 where the old yard track was located. The two-stall Silverton Northern engine house still stands to the west of the depot. The SN depot is just behind the D&SNG depot. It is well-maintained and painted dark green with yellow trim.

In 1949, the movie, "Ticket to Tomahawk" was filmed on the Silverton Branch and in Silverton. The depot was renamed "Epitaph," and RGS engine 20 (now at the Colorado Railroad Museum at Golden) became engine 1, the Emma Sweeney.

(Collection of Edna Sanborn)

On May 2, 1992, newly-restored engine 482 pulled the first train of the season to Silverton, proudly flying the Colorado state flag and the Stars and Stripes as it passed the Silverton depot. (D.B. Osterwald)

Mile
496.9　SILVERTON.
Elev. 9,305 ft (2,836 m)

Welcome to Silverton. First known as Baker's Park, the name of the new camp along the now placid, slow-moving Animas River was soon changed. As one early miner put it so succinctly: "We may not have any gold, but we have silver by the ton!"

Between 1869 and 1874, countless miners ignored the government's ban on prospecting on Ute Indian lands in the San Juans. Some came for a few weeks or months, while others remained to prospect in the mountains surrounding Baker's Park. By 1874, miner Francis M. Snowden built the first cabin in what became Silverton. Soon others followed his lead, and by February 1875, Silverton was well-established and boasted having a post office. The town was incorporated November 15, 1876, thus making it one of the oldest mining towns in the San Juan Mountains. Additional details about Silverton and the completion of the Silverton Branch are on pp. 81-87.

You will have plenty of time to enjoy lunch, visit the shops and historic sites in town before four long—and loud—blasts of the engine whistle summon everyone back to their coach for the return trip to Durango. Try to visit the newly restored Town Hall that was almost completely destroyed by fire November 30, 1992.

SUGGESTIONS FOR YOUR RETURN TRIP:

If you plan to follow the Mile by Mile Guide on the return trip to Durango, note that the mileposts are on the *left* side of the train. The mileposts obviously will be in reverse order. Perhaps there were particular locations you missed on the morning trip, so plan ahead for points of interest that you may want to photograph and enjoy.

As the train passes the depot, Sultan Mountain, elevation 13,361 ft (4,072 m), is to the southwest, and the twin summits of Grand Turk, both over 13,000 ft elevation (3,960 m), are on the left of Sultan Mountain. Directly north of Silverton is Anvil Mountain. Kendall Mountain, on the eastern skyline, was the site of many rich mines. As of 1995, no mines are operating in the Silverton District. Map No. 9 shows a generalized geologic map of the district and the location of some nearby mines. Most mineral deposits were formed within the last 10 million years.

After your train passes the wye and turns south toward the Animas Canyon, a dramatic view of Mount Garfield in the distance is a prelude of more spectacular scenery to enjóy on the return trip.

*Silverton, Colorado, on May 6, 1989, after the second section of the **First Silverton Train**, number 461, pulled by engine 497, arrived. Green marker flags on engine 476 indicate that a second section was following. Engine 476 lost one of its green marker flags before reaching Hermosa. More on the use of locomotive flags and marker lights is on p. 99.*

(Ren Osterwald)

HISTORY

DURANGO

Durango's birth was the direct result of the Denver and Rio Grande Railway's decision to build its expanding railroad system into the silver-ribbed San Juan Mountains. Colorado's mining camps got their start when mineral deposits were discovered, but no real growth was achieved until the railroads, most of them "slim-gauge," arrived to take the ore to market and to bring supplies and people to the mines. As early as 1878, D&RG locating engineers started surveying possible routes into the mining districts of the San Juans. An article in *The La Plata Miner*, published in Silverton, April 5, 1879, stated:

> The struggle for priority of railway possession of the San Juan has now actively begun, and the shrill whistle of the locomotive and rumbling of cars over rocky beds will soon be echoing from the sides of these mountains." By October 25, 1879 another article in *The La Plata Miner* reported: "A D&RG surveying party is now working on locating the line for the railroad in Animas Canyon. Surveyors have to be let down with ropes over the walls of the canyon in order to get the level.

In December 1879, the railroad purchased the Animas Canyon Toll Road from James L. Wightman. The Wightman company had been issued its charter in 1876 to carry passengers, coal, produce, and mining equipment to Silverton from Animas City.

1879 was also the year the D&RG began to building to Silverton with all possible speed. By September 1880, the D&RG had 551 miles of track, and about 4,700 men were working on different extensions of the railroad—an impressive record for a railroad only nine years old.

Earliest explorations into the Durango area are credited to the Spanish, who probed the southern slopes of the San Juans and named many rivers and mountains. Silvestre Escalante's diary for August 9, 1776, says, "We left the Rio Animas and climbed the western slope." His expedition was seeking a route from Santa Fe to the California missions. Preceding Escalante, Juan Maria Rivera led several expeditions into southwestern Colorado between 1761 and 1775, looking for gold and silver. No diary of the Rivera expedition has ever been found, but some of the men who were with Rivera probably accompanied Escalante and pointed out previously named rivers and mountains.

The Animas River has been called Rio Animas (River of Souls), Rio de las Animas, Rio las Animas, Las Animas, and Rio de las Animas de Perdidas (River of Lost Souls) in the literature and on old maps. The correct name is Animas River.

In 1860, Captain Charles Baker led a group of prospectors into the San Juans via the Lake Fork of the Gunnison and its headwaters at Cinnamon Pass. From there, they descended to the open park on the upper Animas, panning for gold along the way. By fall, the men followed the Animas River southward and made a quick trip to New Mexico for supplies. They returned to Colorado in mid-October and spent the winter at a site known later as Elbert, Baker's Bridge, the First Animas City, or Animas City No. 1. The six men continued prospecting during 1861, staking claims in Arrastra, Cunningham, and Eureka Gulches, but left the mountains after the Civil War started, having found very little placer gold. The approximate location of Elbert is on the old map, p. 79.

The San Juans were not invaded again until after the Civil War, when many penniless and war-weary veterans headed West in search of a new life; prospecting seemed a possible way to make a quick fortune. Inevitably, clashes between the Utes and the prospectors and settlers increased, and the interlopers demanded that "the Utes must go." However the government made little effort to keep intruders from entering the Indian lands. In 1863, the Tabeguache Utes signed the vague, ill-defined Conejos Treaty with the government, which only increased the tension between the newcomers and the Indians.

Neither side lived up to this treaty, and in 1868 a new agreement was signed which further restricted the size of the Indian lands and brought an uneasy truce between the whites and the Utes. With each treaty, the Utes lost more of their land in return for annual allotments of food, clothing, and supplies. The 1868 treaty had barely gone into effect when promising reports of gold in the San Juans brought even more prospectors onto Indian lands. Finally, on May 21, 1873, the Brunot Treaty was signed and 3.5 million acres of land were opened for legal entry by miners and settlers. At that time the Utes still had 15,500,000 acres of land in Colorado Territory. When the Brunot Treaty was signed, the Utes lost their sacred San Juan Mountains in return for a guaranteed reservation and annual subsidies. Present-day Indian reservations are along the Utah–Colorado–New Mexico boundaries.

The last real Indian scare in the Animas Valley occurred after the Meeker Massacre in northwestern Colorado, September 29, 1879. Ft. Lewis, a military fort, had been established at Pagosa Springs in 1872. To protect settlers from a possible Indian uprising after the Meeker Massacre, about 600 troops from Ft. Lewis, under the command of Gen. Edward Hatch, marched to Animas City where a sod fort, called Ft. Flagler, had been built. There were no skirmishes with the Indians, but the troops helped calm the settlers. Troops remained at Ft. Flagler until January 1880, when they were transferred to Santa Fe, New Mexico and Ft. Flagler was abandoned.

La Plata County was organized in 1874, and Parrot City (named for Tiburcio Parrot) became the county seat in 1875. Until the railroad arrived in Durango, Parrot City, located 12 miles west of Animas City, had a population of about 500 people, 3 grocery stores, 2 meat markets, 4 saloons, a post office, a courthouse, and a jail. On August 30, 1880, Ft. Lewis was moved to a location two miles due south of Parrot City and remained an active fort until it closed October 15, 1891. It became a school for Ute and Navajo Indians. The La Plata county seat was moved to Durango in 1881.

The first town in the lower Animas Valley, Animas City, gradually grew around a number of struggling farms and small ranches. By 1876, the settlement had about 30 cabins, a school, saloons, and supply companies for miners heading to the high county. Postal service started May 24, 1877, and the town was formally incorporated December 24, 1878. The area's first flour mill was built at Animas City in 1877. Animas City's first newspaper was *The Southwest*. Perhaps the paper's most famous quotation concerned the location of the new town of Durango, as proposed by the D&RG. The editor quipped on May 1, 1880: "The Bank of San Juan has issued a circular in which it is stated that a branch office will be opened at the 'new town of Durango on the Rio Animas.' Where the new town of Durango is to be, or not to be, God and the D&RG Railroad only know. If they are in cahoots we ask for special dispensation." The D&RG ignored Animas City and laid out a company town two miles below Animas City. Soon most businesses moved to Durango. But it was October 28, 1947, before Animas City formally was annexed to Durango.

Rio Grande officials borrowed the name "Durango" from a city in central Mexico, obviously still thinking of their original plans to connect Denver with Mexico City. It is difficult to comprehend today how Durango, to which all supplies came great distances by pack trains, could be laid out in the spring of 1880 so that by September lots were selling for $250 to $500, a brickyard and lumber yard had been built, and a smelter was under construction. *The La Plata Miner* reported December 18, 1880, that many people were coming to Durango from Leadville. In fact, Durango's first newspaper press was brought by pack train from Leadville, and the paper first was published using a tent for an office. The owner, publisher, and editor was Mrs. C.W. Romney, a petite, good-looking widow who put out the first issue of *The Durango Record* December 29, 1880. On January 10, 1881, the newspaper moved into a "spacious" office and plant 22 × 50 ft in size. Her wit and sharp tongue made interesting reading.

Railroad construction continued at a rapid pace. By January 1881, the D&RG owned 3,000 freight cars, had purchased or contracted for 124 locomotives, had 684 miles of track, and the original iron rails had been replaced with steel rails on many routes. Durango was eagerly awaiting the arrival of the railroad, which was being extended from Antonito, Colorado, over Cumbres Pass, and criss-crossing the Colorado-New Mexico border before turning northwest toward Durango.

Every week newspapers reported the number of miles the track was from Durango. On July 7, 1881, *The Durango Herald* duly reported: "The railway is now within 18 miles of Durango and well informed persons express confidence that the track layers will reach this city before the close of the present month." Construction continued at a breakneck pace in spite of trouble keeping enough men on the work gangs, delays in the arrival of ties and rails at the end of track, and accidents. One accident about 20 miles east of Durango injured two men when a blast was set off prematurely. Finally, the first construction train arrived in the "city" of Durango July 27, 1881, and the telegraph lines were completed July 30. The first passenger train steamed into town August 1, 1881. An interesting account of the arrival of that first train appears in Volume I of the *Pioneers of the San Juan County*:

The track reached the corporate limits about 11 a.m. and when at 5 o'clock in the evening, the construction train reached G Street [now 9th Street] in about the center of the city, the enthusiasm could no longer be restrained. Men, women, and children lined Railroad Street [now Narrow Gauge Avenue] for nearly its whole length; sidewalks, doorways, and windows were crowded; the members of the City Band assembled at the corner of G and Railroad and commenced playing lively airs, and this of course brought out everybody.

Soon the officers of the City government appeared on the scene, in a body, headed by the Mayor with a silver spike and a hammer in hand—when all were assembled, our worthy townsman, J.L. Pennington, stepped forward, and with a claw bar extracted the iron spike inserted by the railroad men, then Mayor Taylor, spike mall in hand inserted a silver spike made from La Plata County ore, and with three terrific blows drove the spike clean in, there by uniting Durango by a steel band, with the civilized world.

A railroad celebration was planned for August 5, 1881, but the August 5, 1881, *Durango Herald* reported:

The unwelcome news was received in Durango this morning that the special train of Pullman cars, laden with gentlemen from Denver and other parts of the state, was detained at Navajo by a serious washout, and could not reach this city before night. This seriously interfered with the admirably arranged programs for our celebration today and was a source of unfeigned regret among all our people.

The program proceeded, however, without all the guests and dignitaries. There was a parade of the city police, city officials in carriages, and from Ft. Lewis came two companies of infantry, an artillery squad with gun, and the military band. The parade was followed by various races, a ball game, a shooting match, and the day ended with a dance at the new smelter. Editor Romney wrote of the arrival of the first trains:

> The first freight delivered in Durango by the D&RG was an elegant omnibus for Myers and West. This large and handsome vehicle was placed upon the street on Tuesday and made a fine appearance. It is intended to carry passengers to and from the depot and hotels.
>
> The second train that came into Durango after the construction train, brought the pay car with paymaster C.A. Clark on board. First freight train came in on Sunday. It was laden with railway supplies. Since these first arrivals, trains have been coming in at all hours of the day and night, and no one would dream from the bustle and activity around the depot and the long trains of cars on the sidings, and the incessant movement of several switch engines that Durango had been other than an important railway center for years.

The above description gives a good idea of the early days in a growing railroad town. The Durango post office, which opened November 19, 1880, ranked third in the state, according to the number of business transactions, yet the town was less than a year old. In later years, Durango was the center of rail activity in southern Colorado, with branches going south to Farmington, New Mexico (originally built standard gauge, and later changed to narrow gauge), north to Silverton, eastward on the mainline to Alamosa via Cumbres Pass, and west to Rico, Telluride, and Ridgway on the Rio Grande Southern Railroad.

Durango's passenger depot, still in use, was completed in January 1882. The August 31, 1882, *Durango Herald* included the following: "A lady purchased a ticket at the D&RG office in this city, this morning, direct to Liverpool. We may be out of the world, but we are well-connected."

Across the Animas River, opposite the railroad yards, was the smelter built in 1881 by the San Juan and New York Mining and Smelting Co. The company started in Silverton, but moved to Durango to be closer to a coal supply to process the gold, silver, lead, zinc, and copper ores. Between 1948 and 1963, the plant processed uranium and vanadium ores. During the late 1970s and early 1980s, all traces of the plant and tailings were removed in a massive clean up effort directed by the Environmental Protection Agency.

Throughout the 1890s, as Durango's population fluctuated between 4,000 and 7,000 citizens, two smelters processed ores from the San Juan mines, coal mines opened, coke ovens were built along Lightner Creek,

Whitman Cross took this photo June 30, 1901, looking northwest from the roof of the Strater Hotel. A fire in 1889 destroyed much of Durango, and by 1901, there were still many vacant lots west of the railroad. An original D&RG four-wheel narrow gauge car, minus wheels, is on the south (left) side of the freight house platform. Perins Peak is on the skyline.

(U.S. Geological Survey)

View southwest of Durango circa 1910. The smelter must have been working full-time, judging from the amount of smoke coming from the stacks. Durango's prosperity was due largely to the smelter and to the railroads. Population was about 9,000 at this time.

(Collection of Partridge Studio, Durango)

and electric lights and telephones were installed in homes and businesses. Between 1891 and 1920, streetcars operated from the depot northward along Main Avenue, and in 1902, the first automobile arrived in Durango on a railroad flatcar.

During the first half of the twentieth century, Durango maintained its position as the industrial, agricultural, and cultural center of southwestern Colorado. Serious efforts to attract tourists to the area started when the first automobile roads were built to Silverton and Mesa Verde. Chamber of Commerce brochures proclaimed the wonders of the San Juans, the "Switzerland of America." As highways were improved and expanded in the 1930s, the need for railroads in the San Juans diminished.

After the Rio Grande Southern was abandoned in 1952, an exciting era of railroading in the San Juans was almost at an end. Starting in the mid-1950s, the D&RGW repeatedly petitioned the Interstate Commerce Commission (ICC) to abandon the Silverton Branch, but fortunately the request was denied. The railroad then accepted the fact that it was in the business of carrying tourists between Durango and Silverton on an unforgettable "Journey to Yesterday." Ridership increased each year, but the Rio Grande was anxious to get out of the tourist business. In 1981, the Silverton Branch was purchased by Charles E. Bradshaw, Jr., of Orlando, Florida, for $2.2 million and renamed the Durango & Silverton Narrow Gauge Railroad.

ROCKWOOD

Exactly when the beautiful, secluded mountain valley now known as Rockwood was first settled is lost in the mists of time. It is believed, however, that Levi Carson was the first to settle here, and for several years the site was called Carson's. The Rev. Joseph W. Pickett is credited with naming the small settlement. If it was named for Silverton residents William, James, or Thomas Rockwood, this fact also has been lost. But by July 8, 1878, Rockwood had a post office, and George Warner was the first postmaster. Warner was the son-in-law of James L. Wightman, one of the incorporators of the Animas Canyon Toll Road.

The Animas Canyon Toll Road was incorporated July 26, 1876, and the papers were filed with the State of Colorado on August 19, 1876 by James L. Wightman, Royall C. Bradshaw, Joseph N. Wallace, and Joseph B. Fay. The route was to go from the south edge of Silverton via Animas Canyon to a point in Animas Park east of Baker's Bridge and past the Pinkerton Ranch. Offices of the corporation were in Silverton. When the toll road was completed, it followed Elbert Creek and passed Rockwood (see pp. 43 and 45 for more on the route of the toll road). When D&RG locating engineers were surveying a route to Silverton, Rockwood assumed

Before the RGS railroad was completed to Rico in 1891, the stage route to Rico began in Rockwood, shown in this interesting photograph. Perhaps the group of nicely dressed people had just arrived from Durango and were waiting for the stage to Rico. Notice the rough hewn ties placed directly on the ground, the 30-lb rail, and false fronts on some of Rockwood's business establishments.   (Denver Public Library, Western History Department)

much more importance and was the marshalling point for men and equipment needed to complete the line to Silverton. The toll road was purchased by the D&RG in 1879.

D&RG grading crews started working north of Durango even before the first work train arrived in Durango on July 27, 1881. The grading and bridging to Rockwood was completed by September 30 and crews finished spiking rail onto newly laid ties on November 26, 1881. Passenger service between Durango and Rockwood did not begin until January 1882, however, because work trains were busy transporting laborers, ties, rails, spikes, black powder, and other equipment to Rockwood. No doubt laborers camped here while the shelf track high above the Animas River was under construction.

By 1882, a depot, section house, bunkhouse, and coal house were completed, and the growing community had a post office, school, general store, saloon, sawmill, cemetery, restaurant, dry goods store, barn, corral, a doctor, and a hotel for 50 guests. The photo above shows a portion of this thriving community before 1891. When the Rio Grande Southern Railroad reached Rico in 1891, the toll road from Rockwood to Rico was no longer needed, and Rockwood's importance soon faded. Before the railroad to Silverton was built, Wightman's toll road to Silverton went north out of Rockwood to Cascade Hill, on what must have been a very rough, exciting trip. The March 18, 1882, Silverton *La Plata Miner* reported:

> Misters Ford and Bennett arrived in Durango on Wednesday with 69 head of mules and a camp equipment for 50 men. Working force on the railroad between Silverton and Cascade is being daily increased. By April 1, the road will be opened 6 miles this side of Rockwood, thus eliminating the dangerous stage ride down Cascade Hill.

Track layers reached Cascade Siding, mile 478.4, on June 27, 1882, and crews working on the grade had reached Elk Park. There were 500 men working and their salary was $2.25 per day, which was considered good pay for that time.

A portion of a report written June 24, 1881, by Thomas H. Wigglesworth, chief construction engineer, to officials in Denver reveals his plans for completing the Silverton Branch:

> I don't know what your wishes are but it occurs to me that the best plan is to complete the grade to Silverton as fast as possible, and the track to Elk Park, and stop it there for the winter, prepared to finish it to Silverton as soon as the road is open in the spring. This would give us a chance to understand what is necessary to thoroughly protect ourselves from snow slides.

> Very little is being done towards developing the mines about Silverton. Everybody seems to have settled down to the determination of waiting until next spring and then make a big rush; it is not probable that the smelter will start up here [Durango] before spring, so the ore business would not be very large.

> Even if the mines were producing it, I am satisfied the mines will not be worked this winter now, even if the track was laid up to Silverton, so that under the most favorable circumstances the business would be light, and taking into consideration the chance for serious accidents between Elk Park and Silverton it might not prove a success financially.

The most difficult and costly section to build was north of Rockwood. Rockwood Cut, about 350 ft long, required many carefully placed black powder shots to complete. As the track comes out onto the edge of the narrow shelf blasted out of the granite, it still is possible to see the drill holes for the black powder shots. This section, called the High Line, is reported to have cost at least $100,000 per mile to build.

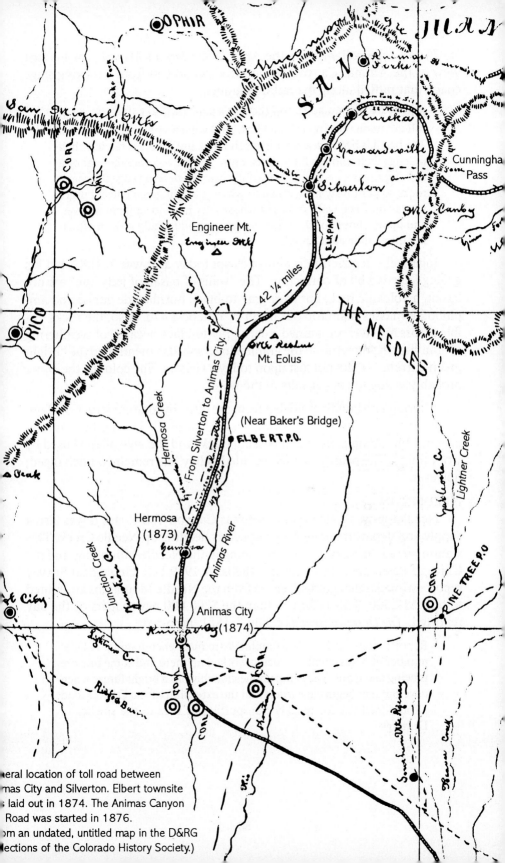

OPHIR

SAN JUAN

Animas Forks

Eureka

Howardsville

Cunningha Pass

Silverton

San Miguel Forks

Lake Fork

COAL

Engineer Mt.

Engineer Mt.

ELK PARK

Mt. Canby

RICO

42 ¼ miles

THE NEEDLES

Mt. Eolus

Mt. Eolus

Hermosa Creek

From Silverton to Animas City.

(Near Baker's Bridge)

ELBERT P.O.

Lightner Creek

Peak

Junction Creek

Hermosa
(1873)

Hermosa

Animas River

CORAL

PINE TREE P.O.

t City

Animas City

(1874)

Ria Baun

COAL

COAL

South Ute Agency

ral location of toll road between
mas City and Silverton. Elbert townsite
 laid out in 1874. The Animas Canyon
 Road was started in 1876.
m an undated, untitled map in the D&RG
ections of the Colorado History Society.)

Ernest Ingersoll wrote in the April 1882 *Harper's Magazine* of his first view of the Animas Canyon beyond Rockwood Cut from a rocking stage coach that rattled along the railroad grade:

> Finally we jolt down the last steep declivity, turn a sharp corner and roll out upon the level railroad bed. And what a sight meets our eyes! The bed has been chiseled out of solid rock until there is made a shelf or ledge wide enough for its rails. From far below comes the roar of a rushing stream, and we gaze fearfully over the beetling edge the coach rocks so perilously near, down to where a bright green current urges its way between walls of basalt whose jetty hue, no sunlight relieves, and upon whose polished sides no jutting point would give any floating thing an instant's hold.

Ingersoll's description is almost as apt today as it was in 1882, but his geology needs a bit of correction. The "walls of basalt of jetty hue" are not basalt, a volcanic rock, but dark-gray-to-black hornblende gneiss and amphibolite masses that crop out north of milepost 470. Also, the rocks visible across the river are stained a dark-gray-to-black because of weathering of iron-bearing minerals in the granite. Ingersoll also mentioned the "bright green current," a fact not lost upon today's visitors. The color of the water probably is due to copper salts in the water.

Although no buildings are left from the busy, bygone construction days, Rockwood is an important station on the D&SNG. During the summer months, the siding is used as a passing track, and the wye often is used by work trains. The beauty of this secluded valley has remained unchanged, however.

NEEDLETON

Needleton was a stop on the Animas Canyon Toll Road. It was also a supply and departure point for prospectors heading up Needle Creek. This station grew in importance when mining in the Needle Mountains and the Chicago Basin area started in the 1880s. A 1969 U.S. Geological Survey report estimated that gold-silver ore from the Needle Mountains amounted to only $12,500. This is far less than the $200,000 newspapers of the day reported. *The Durango Herald* of July 7, 1881, reported:

> Reports from the Needle Mountains are most encouraging. A large number of assessments are being worked up there and some fine ore is being taken out. The camp unquestionably has a bright future when development begins in earnest and the extension of the D&RG road affords facilities for quickly transporting its ores to the smelter in Durango.

A sixth anniversary issue of *The Durango Herald*, December 24, 1887, reported:

> The mountains derive their name from the numerous needle and domelike peaks that rise abruptly out of the surrounding mass of mountains, 10,000 to 12,000 feet in height. These needles and domes are set like mighty watchtowers on the walls of the deep basins to guard the vast treasures hidden away in the great veins beneath. The views obtained from the summits of such of these towers as can be scaled by man, are vast and grand beyond description.

Remarkably, a post office, which opened in May 1882, lasted until January 31, 1910. Earliest production in Chicago Basin was from hand-sorted gold-silver ore that was carried by pack mules down a steep trail along Needle Creek to the railroad. Mining continued intermittently until about 1917, and was renewed briefly in 1934 after the price of gold increased to $35 an ounce. When the Needle Mountains were designated as part of the Weminuche Wilderness in 1975, all prospecting ceased.

The mineral deposits of the Needle Mountains District are very simple, fissure veins filled with gold- and silver-bearing minerals and worthless rock. Most fissures are short, gradually pinch out, and do not extend very far below the surface because the upper parts have been eroded away. The veins are in metamorphic gneiss and schist and in granite. They are low grade, and were never very profitable to mine. But, where oxidized, the values are high. Unfortunately, oxidation was not very deep.

Today, Needleton is a flag stop to let off and pick up fishermen, hikers, and backpackers headed for the incredibly beautiful Needle Mountains and Chicago Basin, where early miners dug for the elusive golden element.

SILVERTON

In the rush to finish the Silverton Branch, much trouble and delay was caused because the narrow canyon made it difficult to get ties and rails to the end of the track. On June 1, 1882, *The Durango Herald* reported:

> Five carloads of steel rails for the Silverton Extension arrived in Durango from Pueblo last night and were immediately forwarded to the front on a special train. The work of laying these rails was begun this morning and we are informed that the track layers will not again be delayed by a lack of steel.

The headline of the June 17, *The La Plata Miner*, stated: "Tracks 13 miles from Silverton tonight." On June 27, the whistle of a D&RG work train was heard for the first time in Silverton. There were then 850 men working on the track, which was 3½ miles from its destination.

Extravagant plans were made to celebrate the arrival of the steel rails in "Silvery Silverton." The town was decorated with evergreen boughs, the 14-piece military band from Ft. Lewis was to play for the Firemen's Dance, and visitors from as far away as Denver were expected for the Fourth of July celebration. An article in the July 5, 1882, *Durango Herald* had a complete account of the day's events. Several excerpts follow:

> In spite of the best efforts of Mr. Thomas H. Wigglesworth, Superintendent of Construction, it was found impossible to lay the track into Silverton by the evening of the second of July, and in order to keep the wagon road from the end of the track in passable condition for the accommodation of the Durango excursionists, it was deemed best not to attempt to lay any steel on the 3rd or 4th. This was manifestly a sensible conclusion.

So once again a railroad celebration was held without the honored "guest" being present. The first excursion train left Durango Monday morning, July 3rd, with about 100 passengers in six coaches. Others boarded the train at Animas City, Hermosa, and Rockwood.

> The run was rapidly made over the smooth track to Rockwood, thence the train began to move more slowly, the grade being heavy, the curves sharp and the track new. The entire distance from Rockwood to Silverton, about twenty-five miles is through a series of canons and narrow gorges, with mountain walls of solid granite rising abruptly on either side from five hundred to two and three thousand feet in height. The mile of road passing through the grand canon of the Animas, immediately above Rockwood, is a miracle of engineering skill and audacity; and presents probably the grandest scenery on the American Continent.

> . . .After leaving the canon the train moved carefully over the fresh rails, under frowning walls of mountains, with the steel grey Needle Peaks piercing the sky above the line of perpetual snow on one hand, and peaks hardly less imposing on the other, with snowy cascades rushing madly down precipitous gulches to join in the hoarse and perpetual chorus of the Animas waters at our feet. Soon we are at the end of the track, about three miles from Silverton, where carriages are waiting and in another hour we are skirmishing for grub in the famous 'Gem of the Rockies'.

On July 4th, a second excursion train from Durango brought about 250 more people to milepost 493 or 494, and they, too, came to Silverton in carriages. In addition to the usual speeches, the celebration included a rifle match, shotgun match, and a rock-drilling match (the winning team hand-drilled a hole in a granite boulder 2 ft 3³⁄₁₆ inches deep in a record time of 18 minutes). Races in the afternoon included pony, mule and quarter horse, in addition to the Hook and Ladder team races. In the evening, the Firemen's Dance concluded the day's festivities.

When did the first engine pull into Silverton? There has been a good deal of discussion as to the exact date, but several reliable references say July 8. This is probably when the first construction train arrived. *The Denver Tribune* reported July 10 that the last rail had been laid, and the last spike driven on the Silverton Branch. *The Durango Herald's* July 11 issue stated that "regular trains have started running", and on July 13 the first ore was shipped to the Durango smelter.

The total cost of the Silverton Branch was $575,366.19. Freight rates started at $16 a ton but soon were lowered to $12 a ton. That was quite an improvement over the $60 a ton for pack train service in 1876, or $40 a ton in 1878, or the 58 days it took to bring mining machinery to Silverton over Stony Pass in 1872. In 1882, a first-class ticket from Denver to Silverton cost $37.30. A berth on a Pullman coach was an additional $4.

Unlike Durango, Silverton was an established town when the first train arrived. The first gold lode claim, the Little Giant, was staked in 1870 along a small stream that flows into Arrastra Gulch. When news of this strike reached the outside world, the rush was on. During 1871, an arrastra was built near the Little Giant, and during 1873, the machinery and a boiler for a stamp mill were transported to the mine in pieces on the backs of mules (for additional data on the mines and mineral deposits in the South Silverton Mining District, see p. 95).

Between 1870 and 1875, more miners flocked to Baker's Park and the mining camp growing around the cabin built by miner Francis M. Snowden. By 1875, there were more than 100 buildings in the new town of Silverton; the first school was opened, and postal service started February 1. Also that year the first smelter was built, *The La Plata Miner* published its first issue July 10, and total mineral production for San Juan County reached $101,958. In this age of instant communication, it is difficult to imagine the isolation that must have been a part of spending a winter in these mountains. The May 6, 1876, issue of *The La Plata Miner* gives the following description of the first sign of spring in Silverton:

> Last Tuesday afternoon our little community was thrown into a state of intense excitement by the arrival of the first train of jacks [donkeys], as they came in sight about a mile above town. Somebody gave a shout, 'turn out, the jacks are coming,' and sure enough there were the patient homely little fellows filing down the trail. Cheer after cheer was given, gladness prevailed all around, and the national flag was run up at the post office. It was a glad sight, after six long weary months of imprisonment to see the harbingers of better days, to see these messengers of trade and business, showing that once more the road was open to the outside world.

The year 1876 was important to Silverton for several reasons. San Juan County was carved out of the northern portion of La Plata County, and the town was platted, named, and incorporated. This was also the year Colorado became a state, and the D&RG announced it would build its expanding railroad empire to Silverton. By 1879, a good toll road over Stony Pass was completed, the Melville Reduction Works started operations, and a brick plant produced 12,000 bricks a day. Silverton was becoming a city. The February 1, 1879, *La Plata Miner* contained a long article about mining conditions in the San Juans:

> The country is alive with mining camps containing the richest ores with insufficient capital to work them. Wages are from $1.50 to $4 per day for miners. It requires an apprenticeship to become a good miner as well as a skillful workman about the mines and machinery. Men can work in tunnels and shafts in winter as well as summer. Digging in dirt and rock is hard work.
>
> The mountains of the San Juan are quite steep, hence miners run tunnels in on the veins, which are much cheaper than sinking shafts. There is plenty of game, but like the mines, requires hunting to find any thing worth having. If women conclude to emigrate, they will push men out of the kitchen and into the mines, where they can dig mineral instead of doing dining room and domestic work about the premises. The wages for women range between $15 and $25 per month. It is cheaper to purchase a good mine than to take the chance of finding one, if one has money.

An interesting description of Silverton in 1883 appeared in *The Durango Southwest:*

> . . .As night darkens, the street scene changes from the work and traffic of the day and assumes quite a festive tone. Sweetly thrilling peals of music are borne upon the night air, and the brilliantly lighted, palatial saloons are thronged by the sportive element, with the pleasure seeking and curious, all classes mingling happily. The sharper with his trap-game laid for the sucker just fresh from the hills with too much dust or bullion certificates, or the greeny from the east with more of the Pop's bond coupons than he has of Ma's wit; either may be enticed by the glowing allurement.

Silverton was becoming very much a part of the "outside world," and it was possible to ride a through train from Silverton to Denver in 29 hours and 50 minutes—if the train was on time. Silverton was hard hit by the Panic of 1893 when the price of silver plunged from $1.05 per ounce to $0.63 per ounce. Ten large mines in the Silverton mining district closed, and 1,000 men were thrown out of work. Mines that produced some gold and minor amounts of other metals managed to survive that turbulent period.

By 1885, the population of Silverton had grown to approximately 2,000, and Otto Mears' toll road to Ouray was doing a brisk business. Often called the "Pathfinder of the San Juans," Mears decided in 1887 to build railroads instead of toll roads. He was the driving force behind the Silverton Railroad, a little line built to serve the rich mining camps of Chattanooga, Red Mountain, and Ironton, located north of Silverton. The narrow gauge rails reached Ironton in the fall of 1888, and the line did a thriving business until 1896, when the richest ores of the Yankee Girl and Guston played out and the mines closed, partly as a result of the Silver Panic of 1893. The line limped along until 1926, when it was dismantled.

Mears' next railroad venture was a line from Silverton to Mineral Point, and possibly across the Continental Divide to Lake City. This railroad, The Silverton Northern, started from Silverton in April 1896 and reached Eureka in June of that year. It wasn't until the early 1900s that the line was extended to Animas Forks. The Silverton Northern continued in operation, sometimes intermittently, until 1942, when the company's three engines were sent to the U.S. Army in Alaska and the track was removed.

The Silverton, Gladstone, and Northerly Railroad was not started by Mears, but in 1913 he took control of the company. The little line, just 7 miles, ran up Cement Creek to the mining camp of Gladstone. Track laying started in April 1899, and reached Gladstone by July. The line was dismantled in 1938. Map No. 9 (p. 65) shows the location of these three lines.

Silverton's economical well-being, like that of most mining camps in Colorado, was influenced by events elsewhere. National financial panics, depressions, wars, weather, and the fluctuating price of metals affected each and every citizen. Through the years, new strikes were made, and companies were organized, sold, reorganized; some went bankrupt. Smelters and concentrating plants were built and operated until the price of concentrates became too low to make a profit. Floods, fires, flu epidemics, labor strikes, accidents, and the difficulties of working at elevations of 13,000 feet made mining in the high, rugged San Juan Mountains a real challenge.

Of the hundreds of large, well-known mines in the district, perhaps the best known and most productive one was the Sunnyside Mine. It was discovered in 1873 by Reuben J. McNutt and George Howard in a cirque basin between Hanson Peak and Bonita Peak, above the headwaters of Eureka Gulch and Lake Emma. Through the years, the mine was sold, resold, and experienced several bankruptcy proceedings. In 1915, a new flotation process to extract the lead, zinc, copper, and silver was perfected, and the following year a flotation mill was built at Eureka. By 1927, the Sunnyside became the first mine in Colorado to produce 1,000 tons of ore per day. But the stock market crash of 1929 brought all operations to a halt

Silverton in 1909, from the lower slope of Anvil Mountain, looking southwest toward Sultan Mountain. In the foreground is the track of the Silverton Northern Railroad. Mineral Creek and the track for the Silverton Railroad are barely visible in the middle ground at the far left, and the Silverton Gladstone & Northerly Railroad track, which went up Cement Creek, is in the middle ground on the right.

(L.C. McClure, Denver Public Library, Western History Department)

George L. Beam, D&RG photographer, captured this interesting view of Greene Street in Silverton. The year is 1910, and the city hall, on the left, is three years old. Sultan Mountain is on the skyline.   (Denver Public Library, Western History Department)

the following year. Sunnyside did not resume any mining until 1937. Only the Shenandoah-Dives mine, located high on the eastern slope of Little Giant Peak, kept Silverton from becoming a ghost town. The Shenandoah-Dives mill also processed Sunnyside ores in later years.

In 1959, in an attempt to increase production of known ore reserves of the Sunnyside veins, the American Tunnel was reopened and extended eastward. This tunnel started near the Gold King Mine at Gladstone. Large bodies of profitable gold-bearing lead-zinc ores were found. But tragedy struck in 1974 when melting snows breached a tailing pond north of Silverton, releasing 100,000 tons of gray slime onto a state highway and into the Animas River above Silverton. The cleanup took almost a month and all mining was shut down. On June 4, 1971, another disaster of major proportions struck. Water in Lake Emma seeped down through cracks to an exploratory borehole being drilled about 70 ft below the lake's surface, and soon the entire lake was drained into the mine. The American Tunnel was completely filled with mud. Fortunately, the break occurred on a Sunday, or more than 125 men would have lost their lives. It took two years to clean all the mud from the tunnels and resume mining operations, and the efforts forced the company into bankruptcy. In 1985, the company, Standard Metals, sold the Sunnyside mine to Echo Bay Mines, a Canadian gold mining company. But Echo Bay could not make a profit and shut down all mining in the Sunnyside mine in 1991. San Juan County immediately had the largest unemployment rate of any county in the state. In its day, the old Sunnyside mine produced more than 6 million tons of ore from 95 miles of underground workings.

The National Park Service designated Silverton a National Historical Landmark in 1962. A bronze plaque is mounted on the wall of the old jail. Today (1995), Silverton continues to remember and reflect on its rich mining heritage, even though the town is now largely dependent upon the visitors that arrive each summer day on the D&SNG Railroad.

SUMMARY OF ANIMAS CANYON GEOLOGY

The San Juan Mountains probably contain as great a variety of geo-logic structures, rocks, minerals, geomorphic features, and magnificent scenery as any mountain range in Colorado. From the oldest Precambrian rocks in the Animas Canyon to the red, oxidized Tertiary volcanic rocks in peaks of the Silverton area, to the beautiful, glaciated horns of the Needle Mountains, the geology is doubly interesting because of the ease with which these features can be seen.

Geologic events in the Precambrian Era, which ended some 570 million years ago, are much more difficult to decipher and understand than geologic events and processes which occurred during the Late Quaternary Period, which began only 2 million years ago. The major events in each era of geologic time are summarized briefly below.

PROTEROZOIC HISTORY

Four major units of Precambrian Period rocks have been identified and named in the Animas Canyon. The oldest are ancient, highly metamor-phosed gneisses, schists, granite gneisses, and amphibolites of unknown origin. These ancient rocks were folded, faulted, and subjected to extreme heat and pressure during several stages of mountain building. Later they were uplifted and exposed to erosion. The gabbro which crops out near milepost 475 is a dark, medium- to coarse-grained igneous rock that was intruded (injected or emplaced) into the older gneisses and schists. The third sequence of Precambrian rocks is the Uncompahgre Formation. It is composed of quartzites and conglomerates which were laid down as sand and gravel by rivers upon a newly formed, submerged erosion surface cut on the old gneisses and schists. These Uncompahgre rocks were metamor-phosed into hard quartzites, slates, and schists that now are exposed near Elk Park. During late Precambrian time, granitic rocks were injected into the gneisses and schists as hot, fluid masses which gradually cooled into solid granite. These granites are classified according to their minerals and age. As shown on the Geologic Column, pp. 90-91, Twilight Granite is the oldest, followed by Tenmile, Whitehead, Eolus, and Trimble Granites. The oldest Precambrian granites have been metamorphosed to granite gneisses.

PALEOZOIC HISTORY

At the end of Precambrian Period, the San Juan Mountains were eroded to a rather smooth, rolling plain that was gradually submerged beneath a shallow sea. During Cambrian time, the material that was brought into this sea by ancient rivers was deposited on the beveled surface of the Pre-cambrian rocks in the form of a thin layer of sandstone and conglomerate that was compacted and cemented into the Ignacio Quartzite. Marine sedi-ments were laid down beneath the sea during the Ordovician, Silurian, and Lower Devonian Periods, but all of these deposits were removed by erosion, leaving only remnants of the Ignacio. Later, the widespread marine Elbert Formation and the Ouray Limestone were deposited above the Ignacio. A time of uplift followed the deposition of the marine Leadville Limestone, as shown by the sporadic distribution of the Leadville, and by its upper surface, which is deeply weathered and which contains sinkholes and caves filled with red muds that later hardened into the Molas Formation.

During the Pennsylvanian Period, thick marine sediments (Hermosa Group) were deposited discontinuously over a long period in the San Juans. This has been deduced by the types of rocks and fossils found in those sedimentary rocks. Conditions changed early in the Permian Period. Marine limestones and shallow water clastic sediments were no longer deposited, but streams flowing from distant mountains in an ancient desert deposited some 2,500 ft of red conglomerates, shales, sandstones, and siltstones, termed the Rico, Cutler, and the lower part of the Upper Triassic Dolores Formations. The red shales probably formed as clay and silt settled out on the flood plains of sluggish streams that may have drained to southeastern New Mexico and west Texas. The color of these "redbeds" is mainly iron hydroxide, which results from the rusting of iron-bearing minerals, chiefly magnetite. The iron hydroxide forms a thin coating on the grains of sand and clay, and is mixed with the cement that holds the grains together. As a result, the rock is intensely colored, but the coloring material constitutes less than 1% of the rock. From 3,300 to 4,600 ft of sediments of Paleozoic Era were deposited and gradually compacted and cemented into the rocks we find today.

MESOZOIC HISTORY

Mesozoic Era rocks are more than 8,600 ft thick in the area between Durango and Silverton, and consist of alternating marine and non-marine deposits. The Dolores Formation, part of which is of upper Triassic age, represents a resumption of the "redbed" terrestrial deposition started during the Permian Period. Jurassic rocks consist of non-marine Entrada Formation, the Wanakah Formation, Junction Creek Sandstone, and the Morrison Formation. The Entrada is a distinctive, massive, cross-bedded white sandstone that was deposited in dunes that had little, if any, vegetation to hold the blowing sand. During the Cretaceous Period, great forests of deciduous trees, which were a source of food for the dinosaurs, grew in abundance and were the source material for most of the thick coal deposits formed during this period. Periodically, ancient seas encroached upon the low land to deposit the marine shales, limestones, marls, and sandstones. The coal beds near Durango formed in lagoons and swamps, and are either above or below these marine sandstones, depending upon whether the sea was advancing or retreating from the land. Toward the end of the Cretaceous Period, the region was worn to a plain, nearly at sea level. At the

Geologic Column For Animas Canyon Area

Era	Period	Symbol Used on Maps	Formation Name	Thickness in Feet	Description of Formation
CENOZOIC (Recent Life)	**QUATERNARY**	Qal			Alluvium. Loose rock deposits along stream channels.
		Qg			Pediments and terrace gravels.
		Qls			Landslides. Loose rock and soil from cliffs and slopes above slide.
		Qm			Moraines. Loose rock debris left by retreating glaciers.
			Ended 2 million years ago		
	TERTIARY	Ti	Quartz monzonite stock; dikes of andesite, latite, granite porphyry, and rhyolite		Intrusive volcanic rocks—dikes, sills, batholiths, stocks.
		Tv	Pyroxene-quartz Latite — Silverton Volcanic Series	1000	Extrusive volcanic rocks—flows, tuffs, breccias.
			Burns quartz Latite — Silverton Volcanic Series	1200	
			Eureka Rhyolite — Silverton Volcanic Series	1800	
			San Juan Tuff	500	Water-laid tuffs, agglomerates, small flows.
MESOZOIC (Middle Life)	**CRETACEOUS**		*Ended 66 million years ago*		
			McDermott Formation	250-300	These Upper Cretaceous formations do not appear on any of the guide maps.
			Kirkland Shale		
			Farmington Sandstone	1200	
			Fruitland Formation	350-530	
			Pictured Cliffs Sandstone	200-300	
		Kmv	Mesaverde Group Cliff House Sandstone	300-350	Gray, marine, cliff-forming, calcareous sandstone that weathers to a rusty yellow-brown and red-brown color. Some sandy shale.
			Menefee Formation	125-630	Gray and black shale and cross-bedded sandstone. Coal near top and bottom of formation.
			Point Lookout Sandstone	400	Upper part is buff to white, massive sandstone. Lower part is thin, interbedded sandstones and shales.
		Km	Mancos Shale	1900-2200	Dark gray to black, thin-bedded, marine shale with some limestone and calcareous shale layers.
		Kd	Dakota Sandstone	200	Hard, brown, cliff-forming sandstones, with interbedded carbonaceous shale, conglomeratic sandstone and coal beds.
	JURASSIC		*Ended 144 million years ago*		
		J	Morrison Formation Brushy Basin Member	500	Greenish-gray to maroon bentonitic shale and mudstone interbedded with thin, greenish to gray sandstone beds.
			Salt Wash Member		Gray to brown sandstone with some interbedded red to gray shale.
			Junction Creek Sandstone	150	Cliff-forming, white to buff, cross-bedded sandstone with some arkosic sandstone and shale.
			Wanakah Formation	50	Made up of several members consisting of layers of reddish-gray sandstone, shale, and marl. At the base, 2-3' of dark gray to black limestone (Pony Express).
			Entrada Formation	200	White, cross-bedded, massive sandstone.

Geologic Column For Animas Canyon Area

Era	Period	Symbol Used on Maps	Formation Name	Thickness in Feet	Description of Formation
Mesozoic (Middle Life)	UPPER TRIASSIC		Dolores Formation	400-600 near Durango; 40-100 near Ouray	Red, pink, purplish, and gray mudstone, siltstone, shale, and sandstone with fossiliferous conglomerate near base.
PALEOZOIC (Ancient Life)	PERMIAN	R	Cutler "Redbeds"	1900	Dull to purplish red, coarse-grained arkosic sandstones and conglomerates interbedded with fine-grained limy shales, mudstones, and calcareous red shales.
			Rico Formation (or Basal Cutler)	100-165	Red to gray-green to maroon, arkosic sandstone, limestone, and silty claystone.
	PENNSYLVANIAN		*Ended 245 million years ago*		
		Ph	Hermosa Group Honaker Trail Formation	630-680	Interbedded light gray and reddish arkosic sandstones, gray calcareous siltstones, and fossiliferous limestones.
			Paradox Formation	500-1300	Dark gray to black shale, green to brown micaceous sandstone, some siltstone, evaporites, shale, and limestone.
			Pinkerton Trail Formation	0-200	Dark gray siliceous, fossiliferous limestone, and some interbedded gray silty shale.
	Lower Mississippian	Pm	Molas Formation (locally present)	50-100	Red calcareous, fossiliferous shale with limestone and chert nodules. Some sandstone and siltstone. Fills sinkholes in the Leadville Limestone.
			Leadville Limestone (locally present)	100 at Rockwood; thins southward	Light gray fossiliferous limestone with chert nodules, oolite, and some dolomite near base at Rockwood quarry.
	Upper Devonian	D	*Ended 360 million years ago*		
			Ouray Limestone	70 at Rockwood quarry	White to buff to gray limestone and dolomite and some green shale partings.
			Elbert Formation	40-55	Gray, green, red, and purple shale; tan dolomite; red to white siliceous sandstone.
	Upper Cambrian	€i	*Ended 505 million years ago*		
			Ignacio Quartzite	70 at Baker's Bridge	White, pink, and red fine-grained, thin-bedded quartzite or siliceous sandstone with conglomerate lenses and same sandy shale.
PROTEROZOIC (Before Life)	PRECAMBRIAN		*Ended 570 million years ago*		
		pCg	Trimble Granite		Fine-grained gray biotite granite.
			Eolus Granite		Coarse, pink hornblende-biotite granite.
			Whitehead Granite		Reddish-pink biotite granite.
			Tenmile Granite		Pink and gray biotite granite.
			Twilight Granite		Light grayish-pink gneissic granite.
		pCu	Uncompahgre Formation	5500	Massive, white or gray quartzite, locally congolmeratic with some dark slate and schist.
		pCgb	Gabbro		Medium to very coarse grained instrusive rock that cuts the older gneisses and schists.
		pCsg	Ancient granite gneiss, quart-mica schist, amphibolite, gneiss		Finely foliated metamorphic rocks of unknown origin.

end of the Cretaceous, the San Juan area again was uplifted and the previously deposited sedimentary and igneous rocks again were eroded. The Cretaceous Period ended about 65 million years ago.

CENOZOIC HISTORY

The modern San Juan Mountains evolved during the Tertiary and Quaternary Periods. During Early Eocene time, some 50 million years ago, the Paleozoic and Mesozoic rocks were bent upward by regional doming so that they now slope away from the center of the dome, the Needle Mountains. The doming probably raised the mountains to at least 10,000 ft above the surrounding plains, and is the reason we see successively older and older rocks dipping beneath the surface as the train goes from Durango to Rockwood.

Starting in Early Oligocene time, the first of three major episodes of volcanism deposited layered eruptive materials totaling almost 1   miles thick in the San Juan dome. Each period of eruption was followed by subsidence that created the San Juan volcanic depression, about 15 miles wide and 30 miles long. Major calderas at Silverton, Lake City, and other sites formed within the older depression. During Late Oligocene time, metallic ore minerals were injected into the fractures, ring dikes, and faults surrounding the calderas.

The ore deposits of the South Silverton district occur in veins of a complex fracture zone that is south and southeast of the ring faults, which roughly mark the southern boundary of the Silverton Caldera. The ring fault zone contains many veins, but most veins were not productive. The fractures that controlled ore deposition can be classified into three systems: 1) unmineralized concentric fractures and dikes that parallel the border of the subsided Silverton Caldera, 2) mineralized northwest shear fractures and north-northwest trending tension fractures, and 3) an eastern shear system of curving granite porphyry dikes. Map No. 9 (p. 65) shows, in a generalized way, the ring fault zone, some mineralized faults, and the andesite and latite dikes that vary from a few inches to broad zones 100 ft or more in width. Only a few of the hundreds of mines and prospects can be shown on a map of this scale. The principal mineralized dikes are identified. The mines at or near the contact of Paleozoic rocks and volcanic rocks are replacement-type ore deposits, which means that certain constituents of the rock have been carried away in solution and other minerals, usually the ore-bearing minerals, have been deposited in their place. Most of the mineral deposits were formed within the last 10 million years.

The transition from the Tertiary to Quaternary Periods was marked by further uplift, faulting and tilting of the mountain mass. Active erosion followed this uplift and produced a mature topography with deep canyons cut through the volcanic rocks sufficiently to expose older sedimentary and igneous rocks. Near the margins of the mountains the streams wandered laterally, cutting extensive erosion surfaces (pediments) that are mantled by thin gravels (Map No. 1, p. 11). During this time the Pleistocene glacial episodes started. The glaciers of the first stage filled the higher valleys. As the early glaciers receded, further slight uplift caused the streams to renew their cutting; the San Juans as we see them today were beginning to take shape. Slight doming which occurred at this time may have resulted from a new magma moving into the area, but one that did not reach the surface. A second episode of glaciation filled the valleys and continued to scour and polish exposed rock surfaces. The last advance of glacial ice, termed the Late Wisconsin Stage, saw every major valley in the mountains filled with ice. The Animas Glacier, the largest glacier in the San Juans, reached as far south as the northern part of Durango (map, p. 16). This final glacial period left the summit peaks of the Needle Mountains and the Grenadier Range as tall, eroded, and serrated horns, and the lower parts of the peaks, that were covered with ice were left as smoothed, polished slopes. The peaks stood from 500 to 1,000 ft above the snowfields. Terminal moraines left by this glacier are found in the low, rounded, hummocky hills near Animas City and as lateral moraines elsewhere in the canyon, particularly where tributary streams join the Animas. After the last of the ice melted, stream erosion continued to carve the valleys into their present form. The Animas River reworked and redeposited the glacial debris and cut a new, deeper channel down through the loose morainal debris in many places. Elsewhere, the stream has followed the fractures in the granite and metamorphic rocks to carve deeper channels.

Even after the arrival of the railroad in Silverton, this was the method of getting supplies to the mines in the high country and bringing the ore to Silverton for shipment to the smelters. The pack train is loaded with mine rails for a mine high above treeline.

(Colorado Historical Society)

W.H. Jackson, famous, "picture-maker of the West," took this photo in 1875 of a prospector's camp on the high slope of Cunningham Gulch east of Silverton. Any suggestions as to the contents of the sacks at the far right of the photo? (U.S. Geological Survey)

View looking northwest across Silver Lake (Map No. 9), a cirque lake in a basin formed by glaciers. Elevation of the lake is 12,186 ft, and all supplies and equipment were brought up Arrastra Gulch (in background) to the Silver Lake Mine, first by pack trains and later by wagons and trucks. David J. Varnes, a U.S. Geological Survey geologist, took this photo in 1946 from the location of the Royal Tiger Mine. (U.S. Geological Survey)

Mining in the South Silverton District

The first successful lode mine in the district was the Little Giant in Arrastra Gulch, which was discovered in 1870 (mine number 13 on Map No. 9, p. 65). During 1871, gold was ground from the worthless rock in a primitive arrastra; the ore was placed in a circular stone bed, and heavy rocks were dragged around and around on top of the ore, usually by mules or oxen. In 1873, a stamp mill to replace the arrastra was installed about 1,000 ft below the mine, and ore was brought down on the first wire-rope tramway built in the region. Production from the Little Giant in 1873 was $12,000 but the profitable ore soon diminished.

The big rush to the San Juans began in 1874 with silver strikes, principally on Hazelton Mountain. The machinery to build the Greene and Co. Smelter was brought to Silverton by pack train from Colorado Springs in 1874. The bullion from the smelter was shipped to Pueblo via pack train at $60 a ton. Before the arrival of the D&RG, ores worth less than $100 per ton seldom could be handled for a profit, but after the railroad started to haul ore to the smelter in Durango, low grade ores could be handled profitably.

The Silver Lake mine became a good producer in 1883, as did the North Star on Sultan Mountain, the Belcher, Aspen, Gray Eagle, and North Star on Solomon Mountain, and mines on Green Mountain. The Silver Panic of 1893 caused many mines to close, but the attempts to mine and concentrate the larger bodies of low-grade silver, copper, lead, and zinc ores continued until all mining shut down in 1991. U.S. Geological Survey geologist, D.J. Varnes estimated that total production of ore in the South Silverton district through 1957 was at least $61 million. Total ore production for all of San Juan County through 1962 was about $135 million.

RAILROADING ON THE SILVERTON BRANCH

INTRODUCTION

In 1879, William H. Jackson, well-known photographer of the West, had recently completed work for the Hayden Survey and opened a photography studio in Denver. Shortly after, the Denver & Rio Grande Railway commissioned him to photograph the scenery along its rapidly expanding narrow gauge system for advertising purposes. The railroad management was so impressed with Jackson's work that he frequently was given special trains to use on his assignments. These trains normally included a flat car that was used as a photographic platform, as well as a caboose or coach which served as a mobile darkroom. There were no prepaid mailers or digital cameras in Jackson's time. Photographic emulsions were mixed on the spot, the glass plates were hand-coated, and the exposures made while the plates were still wet.

Many priceless early photographs taken along the "Scenic Line of the World" resulted from this happy association between Jackson and the railroad's advertising department. Jackson first visited the San Juan Mountains in 1873 while taking photographs for the Hayden Expedition. His first trip for the D&RG was in October 1880, when the San Juan Extension was opened as far as Osier, Colorado, about 318 miles from Denver and 134 miles east of Durango.

Soon after the track to Silverton was completed, Jackson made a trip over the branch, and for this trip, engine 51, a diamond-stack 2-8-0 named the *South Arkansas*, a caboose, and a flat car were provided. At least five well-known photographs from this trip still exist. All show the engine with a large set of elk antlers mounted on the pilot. Two of the photographs were taken in the Animas Canyon about a mile above Elk Park. Another shows the train along the river near Needleton, and a fourth is along the High Line. The Jackson photograph on the preceding two pages is an unusual view of his "work" train on the Animas River bridge below Tacoma.

It was appropriate that the Intermountain Chapter of the National Railway Historical Society issued a special china plate in July 1982 featuring Jackson's 1882 photograph taken on the High Line. The plate commemorates the 100th Anniversary of the Silverton Branch.

Jackson's photograph thus sets the stage for the history of the D&RG, the D&SNG, and the Silverton Branch. The following pages offer data on the engines, cars, and other interesting facets of narrow gauge railroading from the time the Silverton Branch was completed in 1882, until the present.

Departure times of the D&SNG trains are similar to those used by the D&RG in the early 1900s. Today more convenient departure times from Durango and Silverton are used because connections with other trains are no longer possible. The last connecting train, the D&RGW's **San Juan**, a daily deluxe train between Alamosa and Durango, was discontinued in March 1951.

In 1886, D&RG passenger train service to Silverton was on the **Silverton Accommodation**, which left Durango at 7:30 a.m. and arrived in Silverton at 12:40 p.m. By 1919, the first class service was on the **San Juan and New Mexico Express**, train Number 115 (westbound) and Number 116 (eastbound). Number 115 left Alamosa at 7 a.m., arrived in Durango, and continued on to Silverton. These same train numbers are used today for the early morning train, the **San Juan Express**.

During D&RGW ownership, train Number 461 to Silverton and train Number 462 to Durango were called the **Silverton Mixed**. These same numbers have been retained by the D&SNG for the **First Silverton Train**. The **Second Silverton Train**, number 463 to Silverton and number 464 to Durango, also have the same numbers at those used by the D&RGW when passenger traffic increased in the 1960s and a second section was needed. Today, the **Third Silverton Train**, Number 465 to Silverton and Number 466 to Durango, handle the ever-increasing number of passengers. These three trains still are listed in the timetable as **Silverton Mixed** trains. The **Cascade Canyon Winter Train**, Numbers 261 and 262, leaves Durango for a 52-mile round trip to Cascade Canyon Wye. Freight may be carried in boxcars painted "Rio Grande Gold" to match the coaches.

Travelers who rode **The Silverton** in the early 1950s will miss one touch of informality, however. The traditional D&RGW Silverton Branch caboose, with the conductor's oversized coffee pot, was taken off the train as a safety measure. In 1981, a modern radio communications system was installed and a dispatcher began to work in the Durango yard for the first time in more than 30 years. In 1986 the D&SNG began operating on a "track warrant control" system. Similar systems are used by mainline railroads throughout the United States to control train movements. Scheduled trains operate on the authority of the railroad timetable. All other movements on the D&SNG, including track cars and light engines, require permission from the Durango dispatcher.

Operating rules on the D&SNG are as strict as on any standard gauge mainline railroad. Flags and marker lights on the locomotives and last car of a train serve important functions. The locomotive of a regularly scheduled train with no following section carries no flags or lighted classification lamps. The locomotive of the *first* section of a two-section train carries green flags or classification lights, but the locomotive of the following section carries no flags or lights. The locomotive of an extra (or unscheduled) train displays white flags and lights. Red marker lights or flags on the rear car indicate that the assembled equipment is a complete train with operating rights, and tell track-side observers that the train is intact and has not broken in two. The locomotive's headlight always is turned on while trains are operating.

Motorists arriving in Durango in the late afternoon or evening usually become aware of the D&SNG as one of several trains whistles loud and clear for crossings of the Durango streets after its downhill run along the Animas River. A whistle is not just a noisemaker; it is used by the engineer to broadcast movements the train is about to make. The most common whistle signals are listed on the inside front cover. The locomotive bell is rung as a warning when the train is about to leave or approach a station and serves as an additional warning signal at major road crossings.

Crossing

Whistle

The track switches (or turnouts) in use today are different from the original ones. The old type, called stub switches, were simply devices that moved the running rails from one position to another. Today's switches consist of fixed running rails with a pair of knife-shaped tapered points that can be moved from one side to the other between the rails. A switch stand is located at each track switch. A vertical steel rod with a handle that is connected to a crank pushes a rod between the ties to move the switch points from one side to the other. On top of the vertical rod is a green metal diamond, and directly below is a round, red metal target placed at right angles to the diamond. The engineer or fireman will see the green diamond if the switch is aligned for the main track, or the red circle if it is aligned for the diverging or side track.

Switch Stand

During your trip you probably will notice a number of small track-side signals, in addition to the switch stands. Most important (at least on your trip today!) are the mileposts. Their history and use are described on page 9 and are illustrated on the back cover.

Milepost

Other signals tell the engineer when to whistle for a road crossing. Yard limits (the limit beyond which no train movements can be made without orders from the dispatcher) are marked by signs with two blades angled upward. These can be seen near Durango and Silverton.

Yard Limit

Raise Flanger If you are fortunate enough to ride the train after a snow-storm, a large steel plow on the locomotive pilot will help clear snow from the track. Occasionally, a small car called a flanger will be added behind the engine. The flanger has blades oper-ated by air pressure from the locomotive. The blades push the snow from the track and cut grooves in ice and snow just inside the rails to give clearance for wheel flanges. A round, red target on the flanger, resem-bling the red target on a switch stand, tells the engineer whether the blades are up or down. Road engines on wintertime passenger trains are routinely equipped with snowplows on their pilots. A small black triangle with two horizontal white lines along the track tells the engineer to raise the blades on the flanger and the ice chisels on the engine.

You may also see a large metal blue sign (flag) attached to the engine after it is coupled to the train at the Durango depot. A blue flag tells the train crew that carmen are working around or under the train. Until this sign is removed by an authorized workman, the train is not permitted to move.

None of the D&SNG locomotives are equipped with speed recorders (speedometers). In order to maintain schedules, the engineers must use their watches to time the rate at which they pass mileposts, stations, road crossings, bridges, prominent rocks and notable trees. By comparing these times with a speed table, they know how fast they are traveling. Engineers also judge speed by the sound of the engine exhaust—four exhausts per revolution of the wheels. The rhythm gives them the speed. You may also keep track of the speed of the train using this table:

Speed Table	
Time between mileposts (min):	Speed (mph)
3:00	20
3:30	17.1
4:00	15
4:30	14.1
5:00	12
5:30	10.9
6:00	10

Brakes on trains are operated by air pressure. The most obvious fea-tures of the air brake system on the train are the large rubber hoses beneath the couplers on each car and on the engine. These hoses are connected to pipes beneath the cars to form a continuous air line from the engine to the last car of the train. The air pressure for the brake system is provided by the air compressor on the engine. Railroad "automatic" air brake systems operate differently from the brakes on an automobile, which work by increasing the pressure in the system when the brake pedal is pressed, similar to the old "straight air" systems. Ninety psi of air pressure is maintained in the air line while the train is moving. When the engineer operates his brake lever, air pressure in the train line is reduced, causing cylinders on each car to force the brake shoes against the wheels, slowing the train. If the air line develops a leak or is broken, the brakes will "go into emergency" and stop the train automatically until the air line is repaired and the air pressure allowed to build up. Three air gauges in the engine cab tell the engineer how much pressure is in different parts of the brake system. The rear car normally has an air pressure gauge as well. Large steel hand wheels on each car are used to lock the brakes by hand when cars are stored, much like the parking brake on an automobile. The D&RG narrow gauge was the first U.S. railroad to have air brakes on both freight and passenger equipment. The D&SNG also has installed straight air brake systems as a dual safety measure.

LOCOMOTIVES

The locomotive pulling your train will be one of four classes of steam engines owned by the D&SNG. These engines all bear the same numbers and class designations they had when owned by the D&RGW. Steam locomotives are classified by the arrangements of their wheels and the amount of tractive effort available (in thousands of pounds). The D&SNG owns three Class K-28 engines (numbers 473, 476, and 478), three K-36s (numbers 480, 481, and 482), and three Class K-37ş (numbers 493, 498, and 499), in addition to Class 70 engine 42 (see pp. 104-111 for further information on all the D&SNG engines and their history).

Coal and water are the ingredients that make a steam engine move. Coupled behind the locomotive is a tender which carries 5,000 gallons of water for a K-28 or K-36, or 6,000 gallons for a larger K-37. The tender also holds 8 tons of soft coal for a K-28, 9½ tons for a K-36, and 9 tons for a K-37. The fireman, who sits on the left-hand side of the engine, shovels coal from the tender into the firebox through a large door in the center of the cab. The firebox temperatures are about 1,800°-2,600°F. Hot gases from the fire pass through dozens of tubes inside the boiler, called flues, that are surrounded by water. A steam-powered injector forces water from the tender into the boiler, where the temperature is about 390°F at 200 psi. Heat is transferred to the water, which is vaporized into steam. The steam expands inside the cylinders (located low on each side of the engine toward the front) and pushes the pistons, which are connected to the driving wheels by the main rods. After all this, your engine begins to move.

The original locomotives used on the Silverton Branch were much smaller than those used today. Small, lightweight 2-6-0 Moguls and 4-4-0 Americans were the first locomotives owned and operated by the D&RG.

Later, hundreds of 4-6-0 Ten-Wheelers and 2-8-0 Consolidations were used throughout the narrow gauge system. On display in front of the Durango Chamber of Commerce is engine number 315, a 2-8-0 which once ran on the Silverton Branch and elsewhere on the D&RG system. All of these small engines weighed much less and pulled with less tractive effort than the larger engines in use today. Labor was cheap in the 1880s, however, and the D&RG simply ran more and shorter trains or used more "helper" engines. By the 1930s, 2-8-2 Mikados of the K-27 class (numbered 450-464, and nicknamed "mudhens") were the primary power for the Silverton Branch, particularly numbers 453 and 463.

A close look at an engine standing at the Durango depot or in Silverton will reveal several striking features. The front of the 470-series engines is adorned with an odd-shaped collection of machinery and pipes, known as a cross-compound air compressor. Identical pumps hang under the running boards of the K-36 and K-37 engines. These pumps are operated by steam from the boiler, and provide compressed air to operate the brakes on the entire train and other equipment on the engine, including the bell. The long tanks hung beneath the running boards are reservoirs that store compressed air. Mounted on top of the boiler, just ahead of the cab, is a steam-powered electric generator, called a "dynamo" (identified by its upward curved exhaust pipe), which is used to operate the locomotive lights. The round dome on top of the boiler nearest the cab contains the throttle valve, while the second dome contains sand used for extra traction when the rails are slippery. The rail sanders are air-operated.

One of the most interesting and unique features of the locomotives are the outside-frame wheel assemblies. A look under the running board of an engine reveals that the drive wheels are actually inside the frame of the locomotive, rather than outside. The driver axles extend outward past the wheels and through the frame to the counterweights, which are attached to the axle ends. These counterweights are integral parts of the drive wheels on the more common inside-frame steam locomotives such as number 42. Outside-frame designs were used because they allow engines to have larger boilers and fireboxes on narrow gauge track. The side and main rods are connected to the outside crank pins on the counterweight (photo, p. 104), and the forward ends of the main rods are attached to the piston rod "crossheads." Inside the cylinders, steam forces the pistons back and forth, which in turn causes the main rods to rotate the wheels. Valves inside the cylinders are operated by other rods (known as Walschaert valve gear) that are attached to both the crosshead and the "eccentric" rod. The direction the engine moves is controlled with the valves and a large reversing lever in the cab called a "Johnson bar." On the right side another rod operates a mechanical lubricator that supplies oil to various parts of the locomotive. The motions made by all these moving parts are fascinating to watch when the locomotive moves.

Running gear of engine 476, showing rods, valve gear and outside counterweights. Cooling pipes and air tank are just below the running board. The fake diamond stack, added for a movie in 1956, was removed by the D&SNG in 1981. (F.W. Osterwald)

When the locomotives now owned by the D&SNG were new, they all had straight smoke stacks, to which the Rio Grade added cap-shaped cinder catchers as precautions against fire. Several years of drought in the late 1980s prompted the D&SNG to experiment with the "Ridgway" spark arrestor (photo, p. 146), used for years on the Colorado & Southern narrow gauge. The D&SNG version of the design uses a long pipe to catch the red hot cinders, which can be dumped safely when the engine is standing in the Durango or Silverton yards.

All the D&SNG engines were formerly owned by the D&RGW. Except for engine number 42, all are outside-frame 2-8-2s, but vary in overall size, weight, tractive effort, and in the placement of various components. In addition, individual engines have been changed over the years from their original configurations, so each engine has some unique characteristics.

Included in the sale of the Silverton Branch to the D&SNG were steam locomotives 473, 476, 478, 480, 481, 493, 497, 498, and 499. The 480, 493, and 498 were in storage at Alamosa and were trucked to Durango in 1981.

470-SERIES, CLASS K-28 ENGINES

Ten engines of the 470-series, Class K-28 (the K stands for "Mikado") were built by the American Locomotive Co. in New York in 1923 for the D&RGW. Only three of these engines exist (numbers 473, 476, and 478) and all are owned by the D&SNG. The seven other K-28s were requisitioned by the U.S. Army in 1942 for use on the White Pass & Yukon Railroad in Alaska during World War II, and all were scrapped by 1946.

A loaded K-28 engine weighs 127 tons and pulls with 27,500 lb of effort. One K-28 locomotive can pull 10 coaches between Durango and Silverton. If more cars are added to the train, either larger engines or extra helper engines are necessary.

The 470-series, K-28 Class engines are well-known from their long years of service on the Silverton Branch. Their appearance when new was somewhat different than in more recent years, as shown in the builder's photo of the 470, page 108, and the picture of 478 in 1951 on page 111. The most obvious changes include a cap-shaped cinder-catcher on the stack, a different headlight, removal of number boards, re-arrangement of some pipes, installation of canvas curtains around the back of the cab, addition of sideboards to the tender to increase the coal-carrying capacity, and the addition of wooden "doghouses" on the tenders. The K-28 engines lost their doghouses after they became movie stars. The doghouses were used to protect the head-end trainman on freight trains from the weather (photo, p. 111).

Other additions, made because of the engines' appearances in movies, included fake diamond stacks, false coal-oil headlights, and wooden pilots. The false headlights and the wooden pilots disappeared soon after the movies were finished, but the fake stacks remained until removal by the D&SNG in 1981. The locomotives now look much as they did during the 1940s and 1950s, except for the missing doghouses on the tenders.

Before their assignment to the Silverton Branch, engines 473, 476, and 478 saw passenger service on many parts of the Rio Grande's narrow gauge system. The 473 was commonly assigned to the run from Alamosa, Colorado, to Santa Fe, New Mexico, before the track between Antonito and Santa Fe was abandoned in 1941. The 476 and 478 regularly pulled the **San Juan**, a daily deluxe passenger train between Alamosa and Durango, until passenger service was discontinued between those points in 1951. When not in passenger service, the K-28s helped out on freight service between Durango and Alamosa, which was normally the task of the somewhat heavier K-36 and K-37 engines.

480-SERIES CLASS K-36 ENGINES

Ten 480-series engines were the last new narrow gauge locomotives purchased by the D&RGW, in 1925. They were built by the Baldwin Locomotive Works in Philadelphia, Pennsylvania. The 480s have a reputation among railroaders of being the best narrow gauge engines ever owned by the Rio Grande, and one of the most efficient designs of either gauge. Engine numbers 480, 481, and 482 are owned by the D&SNG. Five engines (numbers 483, 484, 487, 488, and 489) are owned by the Cumbres & Toltec Scenic Railroad. The 485 was dismantled by the D&RGW in 1955, and the 486 is on display at the Royal Gorge, Colorado. These K-36 engines weigh 143 tons with loaded tenders, and can pull with 36,200 lb of tractive effort. Specifications and photos of the 480s are on p. 109.

The K-36 engines operated initially out of Salida to Gunnison and to Alamosa. After the track from Alamosa to Durango was re-laid with heavier rail in 1926, the K-36's operated over Cumbres Pass to Durango and later to Farmington, New Mexico. The 480s frequently pulled the **San Juan** passenger train between Alamosa and Durango in the 1940s.

Engine 480 was returned to service in 1985 after extensive rebuilding by the D&SNG. Details on this restoration are on pp. 144-145. Number 481 received a major overhaul at the Alamosa Shops in the early 1960s but was never used by the D&RGW. It was hauled westward to Durango in the last Rio Grande narrow gauge freight train over Cumbres Pass in December 1968, and was stored in Durango. The 481 was sold to the D&SNG and after extensive overhaul and repairs, it returned to service in August 1981, thus having the distinction of being the first large engine to operate on the Silverton Branch beyond Rockwood (photo, p. 148).

The 482 pulled the last train northward through the San Luis Valley from Alamosa to Salida in 1952. It was retired by the D&RGW in April, 1959. The engine was stored in Alamosa until 1970, when it was part of the large collection of equipment sold to the states of Colorado and New Mexico for use on the Cumbres & Toltec Scenic Railroad. During October 1991, the Durango & Silverton traded fully operational K-37 engine 497 for the C&TS's long out-of-service K-36, number 482. The D&SNG found that the larger and longer 497 had trouble negotiating the sharper curves of the Silverton Branch. Details and photographs of this trade and restoration are on pp. 146-147.

490-SERIES CLASS K-37 ENGINES

Three 490-series, Class K-37 engines, 493, 498, and 499, are owned by the D&SNG but are not in service at the present time (1995). These engines were built for the D&RG by Baldwin in 1902 as standard gauge 2-8-0s (D&RG Class C-41). In 1928 and 1930, ten of the C-41s were rebuilt at the Rio Grande's Burnham Shops in Denver into narrow gauge 2-8-2s, with new frames and wheels supplied by Baldwin. Specifications and photos are on p. 110.

The 490s can be distinguished from the 480s by their old-fashioned fluted (indented) sand and steam domes and by the straight profiles of their boiler tops. These are the heaviest narrow gauge engines. When rebuilt from standard gauge C-41s, they weighed 154 tons with loaded tenders and could pull with 37,100 lb of effort. Look under the tender of a 490-series engine to see evidence of their history—the tender wheels were simply moved closer together to fit narrow gauge track, using the original axles and truck side-frames.

The 497 was overhauled by the D&SNG during the winter of 1983-84. On June 6, 1984, a historic and noteworthy event took place when engine 497 made its first trip to Silverton (photo, p. 148). This was the first time any K-37 had ever run on the Silverton Branch, and the first time any K-37 had run in 16 years. Engine 497 went into regular service on the D&SNG June 15, 1984. In October 1991, the 497 was traded to the C&TS for engine 482 (see pp. 146-147).

ENGINE 42

The D&SNG acquired ex-Rio Grande Southern engine 42 in 1983, returning it to Durango after an absence of 30 years (photo, p. 111). This Baldwin was one of six Class 70 engines built in 1887 for the D&RG and originally was numbered 420 (in the 1924 D&RG renumbering, Class 70 locomotives became Class C-17). In November 1916, the engine was sold to the RGS and was used until the railroad was dismantled in 1952. The last train movement on the RGS consisted of engine 42 with a caboose running from Grady, which is east of Mancos, to Durango. In 1953, the engine was sold to the Narrow Gauge Motel in Alamosa, formerly owned by Bob Richardson, the founder of the Colorado Railroad Museum in Golden. During 1958, the 42 was sold to Magic Mountain Amusement Park at Golden, Colorado, where it was converted to burn fuel oil and operated briefly. In 1969, it found a new home at Monument, Colorado, where it was on display in front of a bank. Engine 42 returned to Golden in 1971 as part of a restaurant display at Heritage Square and remained there until it was purchased by the D&SNG. The engine weighs 35¼ tons and pulled with 17,100 lb of effort when new. Plans are underway to restore this engine and return it to service.

SPECIFICATIONS

Gauge	3'-0"	Width Over Cylinders	10'-5½"	Wt. on Drivers—Total	Lbs. 113,500
Valve Gear	Walschaert	Width Over Frames	4'-9"	Wt. of Engine	Lbs. 156,000
Wheels	44" Spoke	Heating Surface, Firebox	Sq. Ft. 102	Wt. of Tender—Loaded	Lbs. 98,500
Grates	Rosebud	Heating Surface, Tubes	Sq. Ft. 994	Wt. of Engine & Tender—Loaded	Lbs. 254,500
Grate Area — Sq. Ft.	30.1	Heating Surface, Flues	Sq. Ft. 1,600	Wheelbase, Driving	12'-3"
Superheater	Schmidt Type A	Superheater Surface	Sq. Ft. 396	Wheelbase, Engine	28'-10"
Firebox Size, Inside	72⅛" x 60¼"	Tractive Power	Lbs. 27,500	Wheelbase, Engine & Tender	53'-6"
Tubes, 2¼" Dia., No.	106	Wt. on Engine Truck	Lbs. 20,500	Boiler, Inside Dia.	63½"
Flues, 5½" Dia., No.	22	Wt. on First Drivers	Lbs. 29,200	Boiler Pressure	Psi 200
Flues, Length over Sheets	16'-0"	Wt. on Second Drivers	Lbs. 29,200	Factor of Adhesion	4.12
Grate Surface, Sq. Ft.	30.17	Wt. on Third Drivers—Main	Lbs. 27,600	Builders—American Locomotive Co.	
Width Over Running Boards	9'-5"	Wt. on Fourth Drivers	Lbs. 27,500	Date in Service—October, 1923	
Cylinders, Bore	18"	Wt. on Trailer Axle	Lbs. 22,000		
Cylinders, Stroke	22"				

Builder's photo and specifications for engine 470, the first K-28 delivered to the D&RGW, in 1923. (Colorado Historical Society)

108

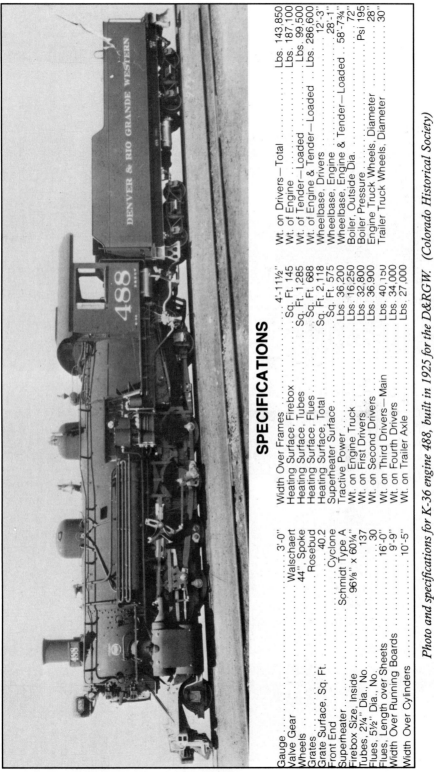

SPECIFICATIONS

Gauge	3'-0"
Valve Gear	Walschaert
Wheels	44", Spoke
Grates	Rosebud
Grate Surface, Sq. Ft.	40.2
Front End	Cyclone
Superheater	Schmidt Type A
Firebox Size, Inside	96⅛" x 60¼"
Tubes, 2¼" Dia., No.	137
Flues, 5½" Dia., No.	30
Flues, Length over Sheets	16'-0"
Width Over Running Boards	9'-9"
Width Over Cylinders	10'-5"
Width Over Frames	4'-11½"
Heating Surface, Firebox	Sq. Ft. 145
Heating Surface, Tubes	Sq. Ft. 1,285
Heating Surface, Flues	Sq. Ft. 688
Heating Surface, Total	Sq. Ft. 2,118
Superheater Surface	Sq. Ft. 575
Tractive Power	Lbs. 36,200
Wt. on Engine Truck	Lbs. 16,250
Wt. on First Drivers	Lbs. 32,800
Wt. on Second Drivers	Lbs. 36,900
Wt. on Third Drivers—Main	Lbs. 40,150
Wt. on Fourth Drivers	Lbs. 34,000
Wt. on Trailer Axle	Lbs. 27,000
Wt. on Drivers—Total	Lbs. 143,850
Wt. of Engine	Lbs. 187,100
Wt. of Tender—Loaded	Lbs. 99,500
Wt. of Engine & Tender—Loaded	Lbs. 286,600
Wheelbase, Drivers	12'-3"
Wheelbase, Engine	28'-1"
Wheelbase, Engine & Tender—Loaded	58'-7¾"
Boiler, Outside Dia.	72"
Boiler Pressure	Psi 195
Engine Truck Wheels, Diameter	28"
Trailer Truck Wheels, Diameter	30"

Photo and specifications for K-36 engine 488, built in 1925 for the D&RGW. (Colorado Historical Society)

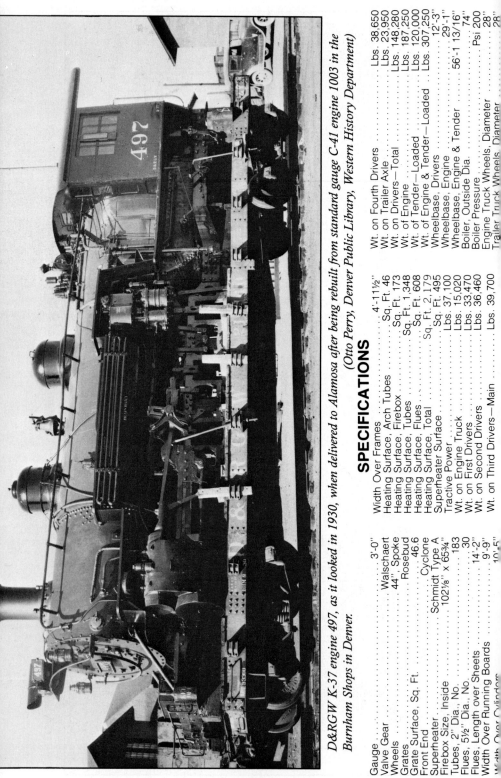

D&RGW K-37 engine 497, as it looked in 1930, when delivered to Alamosa after being rebuilt from standard gauge C-41 engine 1003 in the Burnham Shops in Denver.
(Otto Perry, Denver Public Library, Western History Department)

SPECIFICATIONS

Gauge	3'-0"
Valve Gear	Walschaert
Wheels	44", Spoke
Grates	Rosebud
Grate Surface, Sq. Ft.	46.6
Front End	Cyclone
Superheater	Schmidt Type A
Firebox Size, Inside	102⅛" x 65¾"
Tubes, 2" Dia., No.	183
Flues, 5½" Dia., No.	30
Flues, Length over Sheets	14'-2"
Width Over Running Boards	9'-9"
Width Over Cylinders	10'-5"
Width Over Frames	4'-11½"
Heating Surface, Arch Tubes	Sq. Ft. 46
Heating Surface, Firebox	Sq. Ft. 173
Heating Surface, Tubes	Sq. Ft. 1,348
Heating Surface, Flues	Sq. Ft. 608
Heating Surface, Total	Sq. Ft. 2,179
Superheater Surface	Sq. Ft. 495
Tractive Power	Lbs. 37,100
Wt. on Engine Truck	Lbs. 15,020
Wt. on First Drivers	Lbs. 33,470
Wt. on Second Drivers	Lbs. 36,460
Wt. on Third Drivers—Main	Lbs. 39,700
Wt. on Fourth Drivers	Lbs. 38,650
Wt. on Trailer Axle	Lbs. 23,950
Wt. on Drivers—Total	Lbs. 148,280
Wt. of Engine	Lbs. 187,250
Wt. of Tender—Loaded	Lbs. 120,000
Wt. of Engine & Tender—Loaded	Lbs. 307,250
Wheelbase, Drivers	12'-3"
Wheelbase, Engine	29'-1"
Wheelbase, Engine & Tender	56'-1 13/16"
Boiler, Outside Dia.	74"
Boiler Pressure	Psi 200
Engine Truck Wheels, Diameter	28"
Trailer Truck Wheels, Diameter	28"

Engine 478 beside the Durango roundhouse in September 1951. This is one of the few D&RGW narrow gauge engines to have a power reverse (the short horizontal cylinder immediately ahead of the cab). All the other engines were reversed by heavy applications of the engineers' arms. The straight stack, diagonal number boards and the doghouse on the tender disappeared after the engine was altered for a movie. Compare with the builder's photo of engine 470 on p. 108. (F.W. Osterwald)

Ex-Rio Grande Southern engine 42 in the Durango yards in May 1983, soon after it arrived. (F.W. Osterwald)

CARS

The passenger equipment on the Silverton trains, although they all appear to be similar in external appearance, have had long and varied careers in service on the Rio Grande. The passenger cars were built at many different times by different builders and have undergone numerous and extensive re-buildings and re-numberings. In 1923, all the D&RGW narrow gauge passenger equipment was rebuilt with reinforced underframes, side bearing extensions, and 26 inch wheels substituted for 30 inch wheels. Some cars have survived train wrecks and fires, and others were converted to outfit (work) cars and more recently have been rebuilt and returned to passenger service. A few were idle for decades until rescued by the D&SNG. They have been extensively rebuilt in the new Durango car shop and returned to service. The craftsmen duplicate missing parts after careful study of original plans, and use as much original material as possible.

If you ride in a closed coach, it may have been built as early as 1879, or as late as 1986. Interiors of the older cars look much as they did in the 1880s, except that carpeting has been replaced with linoleum and the overstuffed plush seats replaced with bus seats, many from the Denver Tramway Corp. Coal stoves have been removed from all the coaches, and those cars used for winter runs to Cascade Canyon Wye are heated with a forced-air, propane heating system along the floors. Cars rebuilt by the D&SNG are fully insulated for winter operations. The open observation cars were rebuilt from standard gauge cars by the D&RGW and by the D&SNG.

The origins of some cars are obscure and difficult to determine. Histories of the various cars described below were assembled from many sources, but much of the information was compiled by Jackson C. Thode from data in the D&RGW files. The Equipment Roster, pp. 159-160, lists the engines and passenger equipment presently in service on the D&SNG.

CAR 64

This car was built by the D&RG in 1889 as a mail-baggage combination car. In May 1983, the D&SNG purchased the car from the Black Hills Central Railroad in South Dakota and refurbished it for use as a baggage and concession car.

CAR 126

Car number 126 was built by the D&RG in 1883 as baggage car 27. It was renumbered 126 in 1886; at that time it had a clerestory roof with one baggage door per side and no end doors. In 1923, the car was lowered. Train-line steam heat, air and signal lines were added in 1939 so the car could be used on the **San Juan** and **Shavano**. The D&RGW's Burnham Shops in Denver converted it into a snack-bar car in 1963, and converted car 126 to a coach in 1979 when steel siding, seats and windows were added. The D&SNG reconverted the coach to a permanent concession car in 1982.

D&RGW baggage car 126 at Durango, September 4, 1951. The "Rio Grande Gold" paint was applied for the movie, "Ticket to Tomahawk," but the letterboard at the top had not yet been lettered "Denver & Rio Grande Western." Compare with the photo of car 212 on p. 114. *(F.W. Osterwald)*

CAR 212

The oldest car in regular use on **The Silverton** trains (and as far as is known, the second oldest railroad car in Colorado) is D&SNG car 212. It was built by Billmeyer and Small in 1879 as a coach, named *Caliente*, and its original number was 20. At that time it had a seating capacity of 45. It was rebuilt in 1887 into a combination coach-baggage car and was renumbered 215. At that time it had a clerestory roof with bullnose ends. The interior of the passenger compartment was finished in ash and the baggage compartment was painted a light green. The 212 underwent some changes later, however, because by 1904 the clerestory roof had duckbill ends and there were seats for 28 passengers. In 1923, the car, together with most other D&RGW narrow gauge passenger equipment, was rebuilt and lowered.

The car served the Pagosa Springs Branch of the D&RGW many years and, during that service, a caboose cupola, end ladders, and roof walks were added for mixed train use, as well as high handrails along the roof walks. When the Pagosa Springs Branch was abandoned, the cupola was removed and the handrails and roof walk extended for the full length of the car. The car then was assigned to the Silverton Branch. In an interesting turn of events, D&RGW car 215 became 212. Combination car 215 had been sold by the Rio Grande to a Mexican railroad in 1942, but when the D&RGW discovered that 215 was larger than another narrow gauge combine, numbered 212, the numbers of the two cars were switched and the smaller car was sent to Mexico.

In 1950, the 212 and coaches 306, 320, and 284 were painted yellow-orange (now known as "Rio Grande Gold") for the movie "Ticket to Tomahawk," which was filmed mostly on the Silverton Branch. At that time the high handrail on the roof was removed. Shortly thereafter, 212 became the entire consist of a short train that ran between Chama and Dulce, New Mexico, for a few months after passenger service between Alamosa and Durango was discontinued because the New Mexico Public Utilities Commission refused permission to abandon the **San Juan** in that state. After abandonment, coach 212 returned to the Silverton Branch. In 1964, the car was converted at the Burnham Shops to a snack-bar car. Number 212 was converted to a coach and given new steel siding at Burnham in 1979. The coach seats were removed to provide more space for the snack-bar by the D&SNG in 1982, and by 1986, it was a concession car.

Combination car 212 at Durango, September 4, 1951. The new "Rio Grande Gold" paint job was done for the movie, "Ticket to Tomahawk." Another photo of this coach is on p. 140. *(F. W. Osterwald)*

CAR 213

Combination car 213, named *Home Ranch*, was built in 1983 by the D&SNG. It is especially designed so that passengers in wheelchairs can ride the train. Telluride Iron Works in Durango fabricated the steel frame and wood siding, using D&RGW plans for other cars built during the 1960s. Sliding doors on each side, equivalent to baggage doors on conventional coach-baggage combines, have hydraulic lifts to handle wheelchairs. Extra-wide aisles, a large restroom, and hand rails make this car ideal for disabled patrons.

CAR 257

Car 257 was built in 1880 by Jackson and Sharp as coach 43 for the D&RG. When delivered, it had duckbill roof ends. But these were covered to resemble bullnose ends when the car was rebuilt in 1886 and renumbered 267. In May 1891, it was sold to the Rio Grande Southern, which rebuilt the car and renumbered it 257. It was used as a coach until some time in the 1920s, when it was converted into a passenger-baggage combination car with two narrow side doors, leaving only about ⅓ of it for people; the windows in the baggage portion were covered. Number 257 was retired when the RGS began to operate its famous "Galloping Geese" gasoline-powered railcars in 1931. For 30 years, the car sat without wheels on a farm near Montrose and more recently in Silverton, until the D&SNG obtained the car in August 1983. After a complete rebuilding, the car again has duckbilled ends and refabricated Buntin-type reversible seats. Car 257 returned to service in 1986 as a coach, named *Shenandoah*.

Coaches 284 and 327 in the Durango yards in September 1951 still wearing their Pullman green paint job. Coach 284 is now preserved at the Colorado Railroad Museum in Golden. Coach 327 (see p. 118) has been refurbished by the D&SNG and is named Durango.

(F.W. Osterwald)

115

CAR 270
    This coach was built in 1880 at the Delaware Car Works of Jackson and Sharp, as number 46, and named *Galesteo*. It was renumbered 270 in 1886. In 1924, it became a kitchen-diner outfit car numbered 0270. The car was rebuilt by the D&SNG in 1982, and is fully insulated for winter use.

D&RGW outfit car 0270, now D&SNG coach 270 and named the Pinkerton, *as it looked in February 1969 in the Durango yards when still used as a kitchen-diner outfit car.*
(R. W. Osterwald)

End view of coach 270 in the D&SNG car shop. The underframe and sagging end platform were completely rebuilt and the trucks (wheels), in the foreground, were overhauled.
(F. W. Osterwald)

The interior was restored to its original condition except for the floor and seats. The interior has bird's-eye maple panels between the windows. Portions of the original oak and mahogany moldings were preserved, and new ones were milled to match. All moldings were carefully reinstalled above the windows. Buntin-type reversible seats were redesigned and fabricated by the D&SNG for this coach, using an original Buntin seat in an old work car as a model. The car is named *Pinkerton*.

CAR 291

Coach 291 was built by Jackson and Sharp in 1881 as D&RG Railway coach 67 (without a name). It was renumbered 291 in 1886 and 0291 in 1924, when it was transferred to non-revenue work service. The car was completely rebuilt in 1984. Named the *King Mine*, it has seats that duplicate the old fashioned reversible ("walkover") seats used in coaches a hundred years ago.

CAR 311

Car 311 was built in 1881 by Jackson and Sharp as D&RG coach 87, with a seating capacity of 44 passengers. It too was renumbered in 1887. The interior was finished in oak, and contained 22 Buntin reversible seats, continuous hat racks, oil lamps, and "one large cooler." It was sold in 1944 to the Montezuma Lumber Co. at McPhee, near Dolores. Later, the car was resold and used as a residence. The D&SNG bought the coach in 1982, and after a complete rebuilding in 1984, the coach, named *McPhee*, was returned to service.

D&RGW coach 311 at Alamosa in 1939, when it was painted pullman green.
(Turner Van Nort)

117

CARS 312, 323, AND 327

These three coaches all were built by the D&RG in 1887 with clere-story roofs and bullnose ends, which they still have. They were finished in ash and seated 46 passengers. Each coach was lowered in 1923, rebuilt in 1937 at the Alamosa shops with vestibule ends, train-line steam heat instead of a coal stove, electric lights, and deluxe Heywood-Wakefield reclining coach seats for 24 passengers. New windows and scribed steel sides were installed at the D&RGW Burnham Shops in 1978-79 to replace the original wooden sides. All were used on the **San Juan** and **Shavano** trains.

Coach 312 replaced another coach which originally was been number 88. The D&SNG named coach 312 the *Silverton*. Coach 323 is named *Animas City*, and Coach 327 is named *Durango*.

CAR 313

This open observation car was built during the winter of 1987-88 for use with the Animas Canyon Railway diesel bus that hauled hikers and fishermen from Rockwood into the canyon during 1989-91. It was painted red and numbered 1002. The car was stored from 1992-97 until it was rebuilt into open observation car 313. This number was selected because of the car's resemblance to the D&RGW Silver Vista which also bore the number 313 and was destroyed by fire (photo, p. 140).

CAR 319

Coach 319 was built in 1882 by Jackson and Sharp as car number 95. It had a clerestory roof and bullnose ends. By 1886 it was renumbered 319. Through the years it went through the same rebuildings and remodeling that coaches 312, 323, and 327 did. The D&SNG named this car *Needleton*.

CARS 330-337

Coaches 330, 331, 332, 333, 334, 335, 336 and 337 are slightly different than others coaches owned by the D&SNG. They were built by the D&RGW at the Burnham Shops in Denver and have steel sides made to look like tongue-and-groove wood siding. Numbers 330 and 331 were built in 1963, the first new narrow gauge cars to be built in the United States since the early 1900s. The remainder of the cars were built in 1964. Except for the steel sides and aluminum window frames, they follow the specifications of the older cars very closely. The end platforms are fitted with end posts and ornate guard railings which, as shown in the photos on p. 119, are slightly different from those on older coaches. In 1982, the masonite paneling below the windows was removed by the D&SNG, insulation was installed, and oak paneling substituted. The present name for each coach is on the equipment roster, pp. 159-160.

CAR 460

Coach 460 is the only narrow gauge tourist-sleeper remaining from a group built in 1886 for the D&RG. This coach, assigned to work service in

Car 313 in the Durango yards shortly before it went into service in 1997.
(Photo ©1997 by Richard Millard)

the early 1900s, was used on a D&RGW wrecking train as late as 1957 before it was sold to the Black Hills Central Railroad in South Dakota. The D&SNG purchased the 460 in 1983, but it has not yet been restored.

CAR 566

Car 566 probably was originally mail car 14, built in 1882 by the D&RG, using iron work from Billmeyer and Small. Early D&RG records are difficult to interpret because in 1883, cars were designated as express, baggage, and mail, with each category starting with the number one. In 1886, these designations were changed to express, baggage, postal, and combined mail-baggage-express. Not all the early designations of individual cars carried through to the later designations because of rebuildings, renumberings, scrappings, and destruction by accidents. When former D&RGW outfit car 0566 was being rebuilt by the D&SNG in 1982, the number 14 was discovered on the under frame beams above the trucks. The original configuration was found to be that of a four-door railway post office car when the old siding was removed. According to D&RGW records, the original mail cars numbered 14 to 21 were changed to postal cars and renumbered by 1886. During this renumbering, mail car 14 became postal car number 1—but this didn't last long because it was rebuilt to excursion car 566, probably about 1888. At that time the four side-doors were removed and seats and windows added. As an excursion car it was divided into two compartments, with a table, desk, and two bunks. It was renumbered 0566 in July 1904, and changed from passenger to work service in 1914. By 1920, it was listed as a Bridge and Building Deptepartment Foreman coach outfit car. It now serves as a concession car.

Badly weathered D&RGW outfit car 0566, now D&SNG concession car 566, at Durango in February 1969. *(R. W. Osterwald)*

Although the interior of the new Durango car shop was not completed in February 1982, carmen were busy reconditioning, insulating, and refinishing the 566. To insulate the car, all the siding had to be removed and replaced. The original oak center-sill was replaced with steel, and the car was completely reinforced. *(F. W. Osterwald)*

CARS 630, 631, 632

Three new coaches, numbers 630-632, the *Hunt*, the *North Star*, and the *Tefft*, were added to the D&SNG roster in 1984 and 1986. The steel underframes and superstructures were built by the Telluride Iron Works in Durango; all other work was done by the D&SNG carmen. These cars all have wood siding.

OPEN OBSERVATION CARS

Open observation cars 400, 401, and 402 were originally standard gauge D&RGW boxcars 67191, 66665 and 66271. In 1953, these boxcars were converted into pipe cars numbers 9609, 9611, and 9605, respectively, by cutting down and bracing the sides, removing the ends, and adding narrow gauge trucks. As pipe cars they were used between Alamosa and Farmington, New Mexico during the oil and gas boom in the San Juan Basin in the 1950s. The cars were converted into observation cars by equipping them with passenger car trucks, steel roofs, tile floors, and tramway seats in 1963. Three additional open observation cars, 403, 404, and 405, were built in the Burnham Shops for the 1967 season of **The Silverton**. These were converted from pipe cars 9606, 9600, and 9601, respectively, which were also originally D&RGW standard gauge boxcars in the 66000-66999 series. The trucks for these three cars came from coaches 284, 306, and 320, which were sold to the Colorado Railroad Museum in Golden. Open observation cars 411 and 412 were built between 1982 and 1985 by the D&SNG from pipe cars 9603 and 9608.

Between 1982 and 1986, eleven new open observation cars were built by the D&SNG (Roster, pp. 159-160). Fourteen pairs of passenger trucks were built in 1983 for the new cars and also to replace worn sets on some of the older equipment. Look for the new D&SNG lettering on the truck side-frame castings.

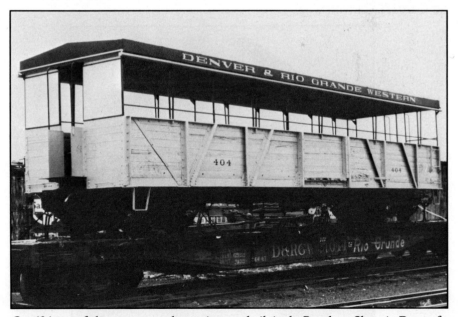

Car 404, one of three new open observation cars built in the Burnham Shops in Denver for use on **The Silverton***. This photo was taken May 29, 1967, in Alamosa, shortly after the car arrived on a standard gauge flatcar. It went to Durango on June 12 with the first westbound freight of the year.* *(D.B. Osterwald)*

SPECIAL CARS
CAR 350

Coach 350 has had an extremely checkered career. The car was built in 1880 by Jackson and Sharp as Horton chair car number 25, carrying the name *Hidalgo*, which reflected the original Rio Grande management's interest in a rail connection with Mexico. It was changed to chair car 403 in 1885. In 1919, it was rebuilt into an office and living car for members of the Valuation Survey who were inventorying the entire railroad property after it was returned to private ownership following World War I. In 1924, the car was converted into a parlor-smoker car. After another rebuilding in 1937, it emerged as a parlor-buffet car named *Alamosa* (with no number) to replace the original *Alamosa* which was destroyed by fire in a derailment on the Rio Grande Southern in 1912. When rebuilt, the car had a closed front vestibule, ash interior, steam heat, electric lights, kitchen, buffet, and swivelled, over-stuffed seats for 14 passengers for service on the **San Juan**. In 1957, the car was converted to a coach for service on **The Silverton**. In 1959, it was renumbered 350 and rebuilt with steel siding at Burnham.

The name *Alamosa* was restored soon after the car was purchased by the D&SNG. During the fall of 1981, the car was reconverted to a parlor car with a bar and small oak tables and chairs for 28 passengers. As an extra fare car, it is used regularly on trains 463 and 464 (**Third Silverton Train**) and on the winter **Cascade Canyon Train**, which runs from Durango to Cascade Canyon wye.

The end platform of coach 350, as it looked in June 1965, with simple railing and markers lights. This coach, now D&SNG parlor car Alamosa, *was built in 1880.*

(F.W. Osterwald)

CAR 3681

The rolling stock of the D&SNG also includes RailCamp Car 3681, an ex-D&RGW boxcar that was rebuilt by the D&SNG in 1984 and is equipped with a kitchen, a bathroom, and beds. The RailCamp car is pulled to the Cascade Canyon Wye by an extra train on a Monday morning and, for the next four days offers elegant camping. It is available as a charter car for groups up to eight people.

CABOOSE 0500

This caboose was built by the D&RG in 1886 as caboose number 1. The following year it was renumbered 0500. It worked all over the D&RG narrow gauge system until May 1950, when Robert W. Richardson purchased it for display at his Narrow Gauge Motel in Alamosa. In 1987, the 0500 was sold to a group of Cripple Creek businessmen who had it on display until 1993, when it was acquired and rebuilt by the D&SNG. The interior was restored to the original 1886 appearance. Similarly to car 3681, the caboose is available for group charters.

D&SNG short caboose 0500, decorated for a special "Santa Express" train in Durango, December 1993. *(Richard Millard)*

CINCO ANIMAS

This car has a long and involved history. It was built in 1883 by D&RG carmen at the Denver Burnham shops as an emigrant sleeper, number 103. Emigrant sleepers on the narrow gauge had odd configurations internally, with 30 seats below and berths above. Sometime later it was renumbered 452, still as an emigrant sleeper. By 1904, 452 (ex-103) was redesignated a tourist car, possibly with the same internal configuration. Later it was renumbered 0452 for use as an outfit car. In 1909, outfit car 0452 was damaged in a wreck on the Rio Grande Southern Railroad. About the same time, a paycar, numbered "F," also was badly damaged in a wreck. Because the railroad employees needed to be paid as soon as possible, the 0452 carbody was refitted internally as a paycar and was placed on the running gear and other parts from ex-paycar "F." When all the repairs were finished, and the cars returned to service, the original 0452 had been numbered "F" and "F," which was outfitted with running gear from 0452, then became 0452. The original "F" carbody is now outfit car 0452 on the Cumbres & Toltec Scenic Railroad at Chama, New Mexico. In 1913, car "F" (ex-0452) became B-5 and was used extensively on both the standard and narrow gauge lines of the D&RG by changing wheel sets at Montrose, Colorado. The car was rebuilt again at the Burnham Shops in 1917 and renumbered B-2 to replace a car destroyed by fire during a derailment near Bell Spur. Vestibules were added to both ends about 1924, and 26-inch wheels replaced the 28-inch wheels in 1930. The car was sold in 1954 and moved to Oklahoma. In 1963, the car was purchased by the Cinco Animas Corporation and returned to Colorado. At that time, an open platform with railings replaced the vestibules, and new Tuscan red paint was applied at the Burnham Shops. The car then received its present name, *Cinco Animas*, for the five individuals who jointly purchased the car and returned it to Durango. In 1982, the corporation sold the car to the D&SNG; it is available for charter trips on the Silverton trains.

GENERAL WILLIAM JACKSON PALMER

Business Car B-7 was built in 1880 by the Burnham Shops of the D&RG as a flat-roofed baggage car, using ironwork from Billmeyer and Small at York, Pennsylvania. In 1885, it was numbered 116, but the following year it was rebuilt for use as a paycar and given the number "R." It is believed that the clerestory roof was added in 1886. The car was lowered in 1930. In 1946, the B-7 and B-2 (now the *Cinco Animas*) made a last official trip over the entire Rio Grande Southern Railroad with noted authors Lucius Beebe and Charles Clegg as guests. During yet another rebuilding at the Burnham Shops in 1963, the under frame and trucks were modernized and strengthened, the kitchen was remodelled, the car was painted yellow, and it was renamed the *General William Jackson Palmer* in honor of the founder of the Denver and Rio Grande Railway. The car is now owned by the D&SNG.

Nomad

The *Nomad* (car B-3) was built in 1878 by Billmeyer and Small at York, Pennsylvania, as a Horton Chair Car. It was numbered 16 and named *Fairplay* until 1886 when it was rebuilt by the D&RG and designated business car "N." The car was then part of an Executive Office Train consisting of a kitchen-provision car plus two dining, sleeping and observation cars. This Executive Train carried President Taft to the dedication of the Gunnison Diversion Tunnel west of Montrose, in 1909. In 1912, the car was renumbered B-2, a designation that did not last long. (The "B" stands for Business car.) In January, 1917, the B-2, along with B-1 and B-3, were part of a special train of important financiers en route to Durango after inspecting various mining properties near Silverton. Near Bell Spur, at mile 468.4, the entire train, known as the "Millionaire Special," turned over. Car B-2 was at the rear of the train and is reported to have slid 50 ft down the mountain. The other two cars were completely burned, but no one was hurt. The interior of the B-2 was remodelled as an officer's sleeping car at the Burnham Shops and renumbered B-3 in 1917, the number B-2 being assigned at that time to the present *Cinco Animas*. The car was exhibited at the 1949 Chicago Railroad Fair and renamed *General Wm. J. Palmer* for the occasion. It was part of an entire narrow gauge train from the D&RGW, which was lettered for an imaginary Cripple Creek and Tincup Railroad. The B-3 was sold by the D&RGW to a private individual in 1951, resold several more times, and extensively remodeled in 1957. It was repainted a deep Pullman green and renamed the *Nomad* sometime between 1958 and 1962. It is the oldest private car now in service in the United States. This car was owned by the Cinco Animas Corporation until 1982, when it was sold to the D&SNG Railroad.

TRACK

Without well-built and maintained track and roadbed, your ride today would be rough—and unsafe. The engineering departments of all railroads keep records, called track profiles, that are graphic representations of a particular section of track. Track profiles are used by dispatchers and other railroad officials to determine the types of engines and cars that can be used on different parts of the line, where helper engines are required, where passing tracks and sidings are located, and where locomotives can get water. Maximum curvature indicates what length of cars can be used, and the maximum grade tells a dispatcher how large an engine is needed to climb a specific grade. The weight and type of rail also must be taken into account, so that heavy engines are not allowed to travel on sections with light rail.

Track for the D&RG Silverton Branch originally was laid with light steel rail from the Colorado Coal and Iron Co. at Pueblo which weighed 30 lb per yard. This was the first steel rail produced at the Pueblo plant. Ties were untreated native timbers that were rough-hewn, not sawed. For the most part, ballast was absent. It is quite likely that the railroad considered such things as ballast and level track to be luxuries that could be purchased later with operating revenues. No tie plates were used; the rails were spiked directly to the ties. The resulting railroad bed was adequate for the light engines and cars that were used during the early years. This track work was inexpensive, but the grade on which it was laid was not. Much of it, particularly in the Animas Canyon, was blasted from solid rock. Today's sawed and creosoted ties, even though shorter than standard gauge, would seem quite sophisticated if they were compared with the untreated ties of the 1880s (photo, p. 77).

Between 1911 and 1917, most original rail was replaced by 40- and 52-lb rail so that the heavier 450-series engines could be used on the line. All D&SNG track is now 85- and 90-lb rail except for some 65-lb rail between the Durango depot and 32nd Street. The only 30-lb rail left lies in the Animas River as a result of floods.

Maximum horizontal curvature on the line is 30°, which corresponds to a radius of curvature of 190.99 ft. The sharp curves used by the D&RG in such places as the Animas Canyon explain why the railroad was built narrow gauge—it was cheaper to construct because the curves required less grade construction.

The *average* grade on the branch is 2.5%, as shown on the track profile, p. 128. This means that the track rises (or falls) 2.5 ft in elevation for each 100 ft of distance along the rail. As noted in the Mile by Mile Guide®, there are several locations where the grade is more than 2.5% for short distances. Although a 2.5% grade is somewhat steep as compared to most mainline railroads, it is gentle compared to the continuous 4% grade on the west side of Cumbres Pass east of Chama. Four percent grades were common on many of the early narrow gauge lines, but all except the C&TS are long gone.

A wye was built in 1981 at Cascade Canyon (mile 477.5) to turn trains on winter trips and on late afternoon summer excursions. New passing tracks at Home Ranch siding (mile 457.2) and at Pinkerton siding (mile 465.7) were built in 1982 to handle additional passenger schedules. In 1986, Pinkerton siding was lengthened 200 ft to the north, and Tacoma siding 400 ft to the north.

The original bridges were wooden. Most timbers and iron work for these bridges were assembled at Cañon City, and shipped to Durango. All original bridges have been replaced with more modern ones of either steel or treated wood construction. In addition, most larger trestles have been filled in so that less maintenance is required, and greater speeds and loadings are possible. A large curved trestle at mile 470.2 burned in 1904 and was replaced by a fill (photo p. 32).

The D&SNG continues to upgrade the track, roadbed, and facilities. New, heavier rails have been installed and thousands of old ties have been replaced. A narrow gauge Pettibone machine (a self-propelled track maintenance unit which can be used as a front-end loader, as a brush-cutter, or as a small crane) was purchased in 1982. Four steel hopper cars, used to haul track ballast, were purchased in 1982 from the East Broad Top Railroad in Mount Union, Pennsylvania. A new, modern narrow gauge track-tamping machine was acquired in 1983, and a ballast regulator is in use. For a few days in May 1985, the line was closed to passenger traffic while major reinforcements were made to stabilize the roadbed along the High Line.

Bridge and building yard of the D&RG at Cañon City, Colorado, in 1882. Bridge timbers were prepared here for use on all portions of the system. The boxcar stands on light rail, fastened to rough-hewn, unballasted ties. *(Colorado Historical Society)*

Another view of the bridge and building yards in Cañon City in 1882.
(Colorado Historical Society)

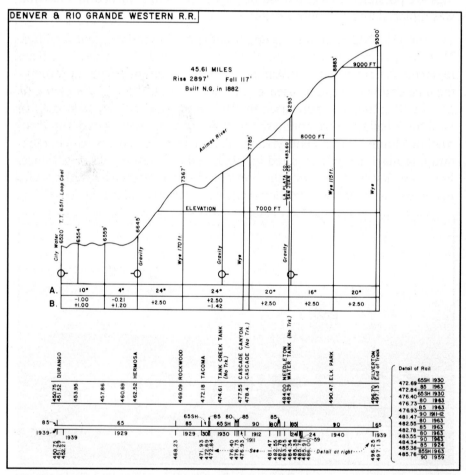

Profile of the Silverton Branch. Circles indicate where water is available. Line A gives the maximum curvature between points, and line B gives the maximum grade. Since this profile was prepared, all 65-lb rail has been replaced with 85- and 90-lb rail. (Jackson C. Thode)

128

CHANGES IN THE DURANGO YARDS

The ten-stall Durango roundhouse was built in 1881 and remained essentially the same until June 1965, when the roof and doorways of stalls 4, 5, and 6 (numbered from east to west) were raised so the 480 and 490 series engines could be moved completely inside the building. The rear walls of these stalls also were moved back because these engines are longer than those used in 1881.

After the track from Alamosa was abandoned, the four western stalls, numbers 7, 8, 9, and 10, were removed in early 1971, and a new roof was installed on the remaining six. The three stalls on the east beside the foreman's office were converted into a machine shop. After the D&SNG bought the railroad, the four missing stalls were replaced in 1985.

This photo, taken during the late 1930s, shows the original roundhouse and the 65-ft turntable that was moved from Alamosa in 1924 to replace a 50-ft turntable.
(Denver Public Library, Western History Department)

129

D&RG general car foreman and photographer Monte Ballough recorded this scene of the Durango yards looking northwest toward Perins Peak sometime between 1910 and 1920. At this time, Durango had both narrow gauge and standard gauge track (three rails) because the Farmington Branch, built in 1905, was standard gauge.

(Collection of Margaret Ballough Palmer)

View northwest from the hill overlooking the Durango yards. Engine 484 was assembling a work train headed for Flora Vista, New Mexico, to repair a washout on the Farmington Branch. Photo was taken June 28, 1966. *(F.W. Osterwald)*

Change seems to be a part of railroad history. In May 1967, the double-spout water tank in the Durango yards was torn down, and in April 1968, the coaling tower was demolished to make way for highway construction. Resulting track realignments gave the Durango yards a new look in 1968, much to the disgust of railfans. Later, the car shed was torn down so that D&RGW carmen had to work either in the roundhouse or outside.

View south showing the double spout water tank and coaling tower in June 1966.

*To illustrate the many changes in the Durango yards during recent years, compare this photo with the two on the opposite page. By May 1968, the new loop to turn **The Silverton** trains cut across the yard track, putting a sharp reverse curve in the track leading to the roundhouse that made access difficult for engines.*   *(Both photos, F. W. Osterwald)*

SNOWS AND FLOODS

Operating narrow gauge trains across Cumbres Pass and on the Silverton Branch was more than a challenge for early-day railroaders charged with keeping the lines open through long winter months. The winter of 1884 was one of the worst on record for Colorado. Snow started falling in the San Juans February 2 and continued for 20 long days. By February 9th, there were 3 ft of snow on the ground in Silverton and drifts were up to 7 ft deep. Other storms followed, and the railroad was blocked for 73 days. Finally, in March, a pack train ventured down the Animas Canyon to mile-post 492 to meet a work train that finally had opened the line to that point. The pack train brought badly needed supplies to town. But it was April 16 before a train arrived in Silverton with two cars of merchandise, three cars of coal, two of grain and hay, and a small amount of fresh meat.

After the disastrous winter of 1884 and another severe winter in 1886, Silverton repeatedly petitioned the railroad to build snowsheds and keep snow removal equipment in Silverton so work trains would not have to buck snow while climbing the grade. Only one snowshed was built (at mile 492.45), and work equipment never was kept in Silverton. During normal winters, well-known avalanche areas always ran, carrying tons of snow to the bottom of the canyon, often blocking the track for weeks. Some years, baggage, mail, and passengers were transferred by foot or burros to stub trains on the north side of particularly long, deep snowslides.

In 1886, the line was closed for four weeks because of snowslides and in 1891, a snow blockage lasted 51 very long days for Silverton residents. Also in 1891, avalanches came down Kendall Mountain and spread out on the flat ground near the south end of Silverton. Opening the track during these blockades was a backbreaking job, and laborers earned only $1.40 per day to shovel out snowslides by hand. During the winter of 1905, many trains were delayed and cancelled. One snow blockage in February 1905 lasted three weeks, and was followed in March and April by both melting snow and heavy, wet spring snowstorms which caused a rash of derailments. In addition, many mudslides covered the track during the spring thaw.

Throughout the early months of 1906, the D&RG was almost completely blocked between Antonito and Silverton. By March, Cumbres Pass finally was opened and men and equipment were transferred to the Silverton Branch, where 11 miles of snowslides needed clearing. Snow was so deep in the upper canyon that trains pushed coal cars along the track as far as possible, then snow was shoveled into the cars so they could be pulled out of the canyon and the snow dumped. To get through the largest of the slides, railroad officials decided to simply tunnel through the mass of ice, rocks, and shredded timber. This snow tunnel received a great deal of publicity

When weary crews had just about finished the back breaking job of tunneling through the huge slide near the snowshed, the Rio Grande sent George L. Beam, its talented photographer, to record some of the work in opening the Silverton Branch. This may have been the first engine to start through the tunnel. The white flags on the engine indicate that it is an extra, or a work train.

This may have been the first scheduled southbound freight train through the snow tunnel. There are no flags on the head engine. The brakemen are standing on the top of the cars, ready to club down the hand brakes if necessary.   *(Both photos, George L. Beam)*

Perhaps this view looking south is of the rear of the freight train shown in the photo at the bottom of the previous page. Some melting appears to have occured, because the roadbed is dry. One may assume the men were relieved that their labors were over—at least for a few days. (George L. Beam, from glass plate negatives in the D&RGW collection, courtesy Jackson C. Thode)

View northward of the interior of the 1906 snow tunnel.   *(Collection of W.D. Joyce)*

134

First mixed train going through the Garfield slide in February 1943 after it was cleared. That year the slide was 75 ft deep and about 500 ft long. (Colorado Historical Society) Combination car 212 is ahead of the caboose.

and it was suggested that the Rio Grande offer special excursion rates for rides through the unusual tunnel. On April 16, 1906, the first train in 34 days finally entered Silverton.

During 1908, snowfall was very heavy, and in March it was reported that water two feet deep was running *through* the snowshed. Snowfall was the heaviest in many years, and all railroads out of Durango were blocked in January. Cumbres Pass was closed January 24, cleared by the 26th, only to be blocked again three days later. As if that wasn't enough trouble for the D&RG, the Rio Grande Southern (RGS) rotary plow broke down and had to be taken to Alamosa for repairs. The Rio Grande rotary that normally worked on Marshall Pass had to be brought to Ridgway to open the RGS, working southward. On February 11, the *Durango Democrat* stated that the Silverton Branch would be open shortly—but it wasn't until February 26 that a train finally arrived in Silverton. On March 7, another huge slide came down near Elk Park and blocked the track. This time, however, passengers were transferred across the slide to a stub train from Silverton.

Other years when snowslides blocked the Silverton Branch were 1916, 1928, and 1932. In 1932, the job of opening the line seemed almost hopeless, so the work of clearing the track was suspended from February to May. By that time Silverton was less dependent upon the railroad for all supplies, food, and coal because Highway 550 was kept open. After 1964, if the main line from Alamosa was blocked by drifts and snowslides, the Rio Grande simply closed all operations and waited for the spring thaws.

The narrow confines of Animas Canyon make the Silverton Branch susceptible to devastating floods. Heavy rains in September 1909 caused extensive washouts, and in 1911, another flood effectively blocked the branch for 63 days. The Rio Grande paid out more than $10,000 in wages to laborers who worked to open the line. Some of the rail washed into the river channel in 1911 still is visible. Flooding occurred again in 1927 and caused the Animas River to move into a new channel in the canyon near Needleton. The original Needleton siding had to be moved to its present location, and nearly two miles of the railroad between mileposts 481 and 483 were relocated.

On September 4, 1970, light rain began to fall in the mountains around Silverton. It continued for three days as a heavy downpour. A total of 4.19 inches fell on Silverton during the deluge. High water in Mineral Creek roared into the lower portions of Silverton, knocked out the new sewage treatment plant, and destroyed the Mineral Creek campground, along with many local roads. The water supply system for Silverton was badly damaged, and water covered the lower end of Silverton for about a day and a half. As a result, all remaining runs of **The Silverton** were cancelled for the rest of the season.

Private property hardest hit by this flood was the D&RGW railroad. From a point just south of Tacoma and north all the way to Silverton, parts of the track either were badly damaged or entirely destroyed. In some places the roadbed had to be completely rebuilt. Gauges for measuring water flow at Tacoma were washed away; this also happened in the earlier floods. Old-timers said that the 1970 flood was worse than the 1927 flood, but not as disastrous as the 1911 deluge.

Fortunately, no bridges on the Silverton Branch were destroyed in 1970, although small bridges over the tributary streams emptying into the Animas were badly clogged with debris. The U.S. Forest Service bridge at Cascade Creek was washed away, however. Hardest hit were sections of track between Tacoma and Tank Creek, in the Cascade Creek area, at Tefft, and at Elk Park, (photos, p. 138). In most of these locations, sections of track were washed completely away from the roadbed. Rock slides were numerous. The D&RGW started repairs as soon as the water receded. This work continued until snow drove the repair crews out of the canyon. But by November, speeders could run over all 45 miles of track. Spring came early to the San Juans in 1971, and most of the railroad was in excellent shape for opening day, May 29, 1971. Slow orders were in effect at some places for a few weeks until the new roadbed had settled and stabilized.

Durango escaped serious damage in the 1970 flood. The Animas valley just north of the city resembled a large lake for a while, but the area is a natural reservoir for high water of the river, and no extensive damage was done except to some roads, bridges and water systems.

View of the D&RG track at Tacoma that was washed out after the 1911 flood. Additional photographs are on p. 39. *(Colorado Historical Society)*

These photos were taken near Tacoma, on September 10, 1970, four days after flood waters receded. The extensive damage to the roadbed and track are graphically illustrated. In the lower photo, the section of track was lifted off the roadbed and left in the stream channel.

(R. W. Osterwald)

THE LAST YEARS OF D&RGW OWNERSHIP

During the 1930s and early 1940s, the Silverton Branch carried a few businessmen, miners, and their families back and forth to Silverton. Freight trains carried some ore from the Silverton area and limestone from the Rockwood quarry until 1930, when the smelter in Durango was closed. During World War II, the smelter was reopened by the Vanadium Corp. of America (VCA) to process vanadium and uranium ore. It operated until 1963, when the plant permanently was closed and dismantled. The VCA plant did not give any business to the Silverton Branch, however, as most ore arrived in Durango either by truck or the RGS. Only heated protests from local residents kept the line open on a reduced schedule. Mixed trains ran on Sundays, Wednesdays, and Fridays, only. But, after the war, railfans were beginning to discover **The Silverton**. Railroad club excursions on the narrow gauge started in the late 1940s, largely due to the promotional efforts of Rio Grande conductor Alva Lyons. These trips did much to publicize the San Juan Extension and the beauty of the San Juan Mountains, and ridership gradually increased. To accommodate the increasing numbers of passengers, in 1947 the Rio Grande built a glass-roofed observation car, named the *Silver Vista*. Unfortunately, the car was destroyed in a shop fire at Alamosa in 1953.

The Farmington Branch between Durango and Farmington, New Mexico, was built as standard gauge in 1905. The Rio Grande anticipated that this outlet to the south would connect with other railroads in New Mexico and carry coal from the San Juan Basin to smelters in New Mexico and Arizona. This grand scheme never materialized, and the "Red Apple Line" was converted to narrow gauge in 1923. It was reduced to carrying shipments of fruit, farm, and ranch products. The oil and gas boom in the San Juan Basin in the 1950s really saved the narrow gauge for a few more years until trucks took over the transpor of pipe and oil field equipment. During 1955, the Farmington branch had the highest number of car loadings of the entire D&RGW system. The branch was abandoned in 1969, and by 1971, the track was gone.

With the dismantling of the Rio Grande Southern Railroad in 1952, the era of narrow gauge railroading in the San Juans was almost at an end. The D&RGW petitioned the Interstate Commerce Commission (ICC) to abandon the Silverton Branch, but in April 1962 this request was denied. The Rio Grande then accepted the fact that it was in the business of carrying tourists from Durango to Silverton on an unforgettable "Journey to Yesteryear." Early in 1963 the Rio Grande purchased a number of old buildings and land surrounding the depot and started a renovation program which resulted in "Rio Grande Land." Stores, gift shops, the General Palmer Hotel and the Grande Palace Restaurant were opened, and a large parking

On September 30, 1947, Otto Perry, one of Colorado's premier photographers, took this photo of the **Silverton Mixed**, train number 461, below Rockwood. This 13-car train was pulled by K-27 engine 463, with the Silver Vista on the rear.

(Denver Public Library, Western History Department)

On a railfan trip in August 1947, the northbound train stopped after crossing the Animas River below Tacoma to let passengers off for a photo run-by. All the cars except the Silver Vista were painted Pullman green. Car 126 is behind the engine, followed by combine 212.

(Colorado Historical Society)

lot was built on the west side of the depot. As ridership continued to increase, new coaches were built in Denver, and the second section of **The Silverton** started running in 1963.

The end was near, however, for the remainder of the old San Juan Extension of 1880. A petition to abandon the route between Farmington, Durango, and Alamosa was filed with the ICC in 1967, and final approval was granted in 1969. Because of the intensive efforts of many people and organizations, the states of Colorado and New Mexico banded together to purchase 64 miles of track between Antonito, Colorado, and Chama, New Mexico, in July 1970. Included in the purchase was a large amount of equipment, buildings, and rolling stock. This portion of the narrow gauge is leased to a concessionaire who operates the Cumbres & Toltec Scenic Railroad. The other 110 miles of track were dismantled, and the remaining cars were burned or sold for scrap.

D&RGW K-27 engine 453 heading north at the south switch of the Hermosa siding, probably in the early 1950s. K-27 engines were equipped with these full-size wedge plows for snowplowing in the narrow confines of the Animas canyon.

(Collection of Kenneth Logan)

NEW OWNERSHIP

Throughout the 1960s and 1970s, the D&RGW attempted to find a suitable buyer for the Silverton Branch. Finally, on March 25, 1981, the sale of **The Silverton** to Charles E. Bradshaw Jr., of Orlando, Florida, was completed after almost four years of planning and negotiation. Bradshaw paid $2.2 million in cash for this last remaining vestige of the once-extensive D&RGW narrow gauge system. Included in the sale were steam locomotives, rolling stock, roadbed, work equipment, and buildings.

On May 23, 1981, Bradshaw, president of the Durango & Silverton Narrow Gauge Railroad, cut a red ribbon stretched across the track in front of the first double-headed passenger train to leave Durango in 19 years. On opening day, more than 600 passengers rode the first D&SNG train to Silverton in the familiar but newly-painted and re-lettered Durango & Silverton coaches. Enthusiastic tourists and railfans filled 15-car double-headed trains during the first three days.

Long before the purchase agreement was signed in July 1979, Bradshaw had extensive engineering studies made of the roadbed, track, bridges, and structures. It was found that by widening some rock cuts and strengthening some bridges, larger and heavier locomotives could be safely used over the entire line. By August 1981, newly refurbished engine 481 was the first K-36 to operate beyond Rockwood. After its starring role in Durango's Centennial Celebration August 5, 1981, engine 481 made its first run to Silverton August 7, and went into regular service August 12, 1981.

During the first year of D&SNG operation, achievements were many. Double-headed (two-engine) trains, long a rarity on the road, frequently left the Durango depot. Much equipment, long idle, was restored and returned to service. A 200-ft long car shop with 8,400 sq ft of work space was built on the site of the one torn down by the Rio Grande. Although the new building looks much like its predecessor on the outside, it is completely equipped with modern machinery to restore, rebuild, and construct narrow gauge cars and equipment. The restoration to passenger service of dilapidated and seemingly derelict cars continued at a rapid pace; several open coaches have been built from standard gauge stock cars. Three stalls and a welding shop were added to the Durango roundhouse by December 1984 (all were destroyed in the 1989 roundhouse fire described on pp. 151-155).

CENTENNIAL CELEBRATIONS

Anniversaries are always important occasions—and offer a chance to look back at history. The 100th anniversary of the arrival of the first D&RG train in Durango was celebrated August 5, 1981, when Colorado Governor Richard D. Lamm, D&SNG Railroad President Bradshaw, and a group of Durango community leaders and citizens rode a special train, pulled by newly-restored engine 481, into Durango from the Iron Horse Resort north of town. A large and enthusiastic crowd enjoyed a picnic, a parade, and watched the ceremony of two silver spikes being driven into a tie at the Durango depot. The spikes were deftly pounded into place by Governor Lamm and by the late Alva F. Lyons, longtime D&RGW conductor and Durango resident. Following the ceremony, the spikes were immediately removed—one was given to the City of Durango and the other was auctioned off to the highest bidder, who turned out to be Charlie Bradshaw. He announced that the spike would remain in Durango and be on display at the depot. Bradshaw also pledged to preserve the railroad, its history, and authenticity so that people can continue to enjoy an unforgettable ride along the Animas for years to come.

Another important anniversary was celebrated in 1982. The National Railway Historical Society held its convention in Denver in July and, as part of convention activities, chartered a special excursion on the D&SNG July 11, 1982. Two trains filled with convention delegates and their families stopped at Cascade Canyon Wye for a brief ceremony to commemorate the 100th anniversary of the completion of the Silverton Branch. A simple monument of Colorado red granite commemorating the "Spirit of Colorado Mountain Railroading" was dedicated by officials of the NRHS and the D&SNG (photo, p. 7). The Silverton Gold Nugget Brass Band provided appropriate music, and the trains carried a special Railway Postal Station to cancel commemorative postal cachets. Other anniversary activities planned by the Silverton Chamber of Commerce lasted 10 days, starting July 4. This was indeed an exciting year in the long and eventful history of **The Silverton**!

In March 1997 Charles Bradshaw sold the D&SNG to First American Railways, Inc., a publically-held corporation headquartered in Hollywood, Florida. As a large shareholder in the company, Mr. Bradshaw has a seat on the board of directors. First American has stated that the company intends to honor Bradshaw's pledge to preserve the railroad, its history, and its authenticity. Because the new ownership had confidence in the way the railroad was operated, very few changes in personnel and operations were made.

ENGINE RESTORATIONS
ENGINE 480

The 480 had been stored at Alamosa and, in May 1981, it was hauled to Durango by truck. Plans were immediately made to restore this engine, which had been retired from service on the D&RGW in 1964. It had sat outside the Alamosa roundhouse 16 years, nearly forgotten and exposed to vandalism and the weather.

When restoration of engine 480 started, it was found that many parts were missing. D&SNG roundhouse foreman Steve Jackson remarked: "Someone did us a big favor—we didn't have to take the engine apart." New grates, firebox door, Johnson bar, throttle parts, and some smoke box interior parts were cast. New wiring, steam and air lines, injectors, boiler check valves, pilot, fountain, and snifter valves were located or fabricated. Many other parts, such as the lubricators, needed extensive repairs. The engine was stripped, sandblasted, and inspected; the flues and superheater units were pulled and rebuilt. Additional parts were fabricated as needed, and the running gear was repaired. A bell and whistle were found in a boxcar of parts left in Durango by the Rio Grande and installed.

Finally, on July 2, 1985, the D&SNG roundhouse crew made the final check, put water in the boiler, started a fire, and carefully watched as steam pressure started to build in this rejuvenated relic of the 1920s. Several more days were spent making adjustments before a trial run to Rockwood occurred July 9. Stops were made along the way to adjust a squeaky lubricator. At Rockwood, the engine was turned on the wye, and the crew poured and squirted oil into every possible moving part before returning to Durango. Few who saw that decrepit collection of rusty metal arrive in Durango in 1981 believed the engine could be resurrected and returned to service. On July 13, 1985, engine 480 pulled its first D&SNG revenue train on the afternoon run of the **Cascade Canyon Train** to the Cascade Canyon wye and returned. Two days later, it made its first trip to Silverton, pulling the 7:30 a.m. **San Juan Express**.

ENGINE 481

Number 481 received a major overhaul at the D&RGW Alamosa shop in the early 1960s, but never was used again by the Rio Grande. It was pulled westward to Durango in the last Rio Grande narrow gauge freight train over Cumbres Pass in December 1968, and was stored in Durango until it was sold to the D&SNG. After extensive inspection, overhaul, and repair, 481 returned to service in August 1981, thus having the distinction of being the first large engine to operate on the Silverton Branch beyond Rockwood.

On May 3, 1981, engine 480 departed Alamosa for the last time. After an overnight stop at South Fork, the low-boy trailer left for Durango at 6:30 a.m. This photo, taken about 7:30 a.m., shows the engine barely had enough clearance to pass through the snowshed near the top of Wolf Creek Pass. The summit was reached about 8:00 a.m. The descent was even slower.　　　　　　　　　　　　　　　　　　　　　　　　　　　　　　(D.B Osterwald)

About 2:00 p.m., the 480 arrived in Durango. This photo was taken just before the track was backed into a sloping pit dug along the west side of the roundhouse. After matching rails and removing the anchoring chains from the engine, 480 was rolled from the trailer onto the track by releasing the winch cable on the cab of the truck.　　　(F.W. Osterwald)

ENGINE 482

Between October 8 and 11, 1991, a historic event, quite unusual in the annals of narrow gauge railroading, occurred. The C&TS Railroad Commission and the D&SNG Railroad agreed to trade the D&SNG's fully-operational engine 497 for long out-of-service C&TS engine 482. The D&SNG discovered that the larger and longer 497 had trouble negotiating the sharper curves of the Silverton Branch. There are no curves sharper than 20° on the C&TS, and the larger engine can pull one more coach up the steep 4% grade between Chama and Cumbres Pass.

On October 8, 1991, the tender of 497 was loaded onto a low-boy trailer and transported to Chama, New Mexico, headquarters of the C&TS Railroad. The next day, locomotive 482 was loaded and moved to Durango. The tractor-trailer called into service for this historic exchange then was loaded with locomotive 497 and went east to Chama. On October 11, the truck returned to Durango with the tender for 482.

According to D&SNG vice president, Amos Cordova, the 482 has undergone a massive rebuilding. A hydrostatic test revealed the boiler to be in excellent condition. The engine was sandblasted, staybolt caps were inspected and renewed, the running gear was overhauled, and intensive repairs were made to the cab, including new woodwork, windows, and doors. Much more work and time were required to restore the 482 than the 480, because many small pipes and cab equipment were missing and had to be fabricated in the D&SNG shops.

After standing idle 33 years, engine 482 began service on May 2, 1992 (the annual opening day), pulling the first morning train to Silverton (photos, pp. 15, 68). A large crowd, dressed in Victorian costumes, was on hand to see the 482 leave the depot on time and ready for many more years of service.

*Opening day in Silverton, May 2, 1992. The **First Silverton Train** had backed down to the wye, turned, and was waiting for passengers to load for the return trip to Durango. On the right, the second section of the train is arriving.*   *(Ren Osterwald)*

*After eight years of service on **The Silverton**, locomotive 497 left Durango October 8, 1991, bound for Chama, New Mexico, and service on the C&TS Railroad. This engine has the distinction of being the only K-37 to operate on the Silverton Branch.*

On October 9, 1991, rusty, decrepit engine 482 was loaded on the same low-boy trailer and transported from Chama to Durango. This photo was taken in the Durango yards just before the engine was unloaded. *(Both photos, Amos Cordova)*

*This historic photo was taken in Silverton August 7, 1981, when engine 481 and a caboose arrived for the first time. On the train were D&SNG officials and David Hughes, who was responsible for the engineering work done to upgrade the track and bridges. The **First Silverton Mixed**, double-headed with engines 476 and 478, is standing on the track at left.*

(David V. Hughes)

Engine 497 pulling into Silverton on its first trip, June 6, 1984.   *(Robert E. Emmett)*

TRAGEDY STRIKES THE NARROW GAUGE

Problems are nothing new to railroaders on the narrow gauge. During the winter, the track often was blocked by huge snowdrifts and avalanches. Mud slides, broken or kinked rails, washouts, and rocks on the track caused innumerable delays and derailments. Fortunately, few injuries or deaths resulted from these events.

In July 1951, while engine 473 was pulling a freight train loaded with 900 tons of silver ore concentrates bound for Durango, the engine encountered a heat expansion kink in the track at mile 483.7 and landed in the Animas River. All the ore cars stayed on the track, and no one was injured. *(Collection of Edna Sanborn)*

Engine 473 is no stranger to trouble. In June 1974, a truck paralleling the train on a dirt road along the track a few miles north of Durango suddenly swerved into the engine. A new injector (the large bronze casting that forces water into the boiler from the tender) and a few other items had to be replaced after the engine returned to Durango under its own power.

Several years later, the engine was broadsided by a truck at a grade crossing in Durango. Needless to say, the truck sustained much more damage than the engine.

If 473 had not endured enough aches and pains from trucks in the past, it suffered a great deal more June 25, 1987. The engine was steamed up and sitting on the ready track beside the Durango roundhouse when an 18-wheel truck, loaded with almost 24 tons of loose potatoes, lost its brakes near the top of Hesperus Hill, 14 miles west of Durango on U.S. 160. The truck careened down the canyon, went through the intersection of U.S. 160 and U.S. 550 (fortunately with a green light!), hit the embankment east of the intersection where it became airborne, and plowed through a chain-link fence before crunching to a stop against the fireman's side of 473.

The scene at the roundhouse shortly after Durango firemen arrived. The collision easily could have caused a boiler explosion or fire, and destroyed the locomotive.

After the mangled truck was pulled away from engine 473, the damage to both vehicles is apparent. The truck was totaled, and it cost between $50,000 and $60,000 to repair the 473.
(Both photos ©Paul Connor)

Fortunately, D&SNG hostlers John Hood and Gilbert Sanchez saw the truck flying toward them and jumped to safety. Remarkably, the truck driver, Neal Fox of Colorado Springs, suffered only a broken leg and ankle, but it took nearly an hour to free him from the wreckage.

The engine was knocked 11 ft off the track by the impact. Once again, 473 needed a new injector. The steel-plated cab floor was badly buckled, and the cab and coal deck on the tender had to be replaced, as did many feet of piping. It took only three weeks to return the 473 to service.

The scene that greeted firemen and D&SNG employees after fire was discovered in the roundhouse. *(Photo ©Paul Connor)*

FIRE DESTROYS THE DURANGO ROUNDHOUSE

During the early morning of February 10, 1989, a night security guard discovered a fire in the southeastern corner of the roundhouse machine shop, behind a metal-treating kiln. Flames spread rapidly and soon engulfed the entire building. All six operable engines were in the roundhouse, and at first it was feared all were damaged beyond repair. Daylight brought hope and some optimism as the smoldering embers and hot metal cooled.

Temperatures near the roof of the roundhouse were estimated to have reached 2,500 to 3,000°F. The roof collapsed and caused extensive damage to headlights, smoke-boxes, wiring, and piping on all the engines. Heavy roof timbers and wooden parts of the cabs also were destroyed. The intense heat burned all the paint off the engines, so quick repainting became a top priority to prevent corrosion. The machine shop was totally destroyed, along with many spare parts that are no longer available. Engine 473 suffered the worst damage and was the last to be repaired.

Engine 480 was in stall number six near the western fire wall of the roundhouse.

Engine 497, in stall five, was the least damaged of the six locomotives. (Erick Nelson)

One week later, all the debris and destroyed machinery had been cleaned out, and a temporary machine shop was assembled outdoors along the west wall of the roundhouse. Some machine tools were borrowed, others were purchased secondhand, and new machines were ordered. Temporary electric power was installed in the open-air roundhouse and the roundhouse crew began repairs. Fortunately the winter weather turned mild and working outside was not a problem.

The photographs at the top of this page and on pages 153-154 were taken by Erick Nelson of Boulder, two days after the fire. They illustrate the depressing sight that greeted heartsick D&SNG employees and everyone in Durango. The pictures are arranged in the same order in which the engines stood in the roundhouse.

Engines 481 and 478 (right) on the morning of February 12, 1989.   *(Erick Nelson)*

Two views of the machine shop along the north wall of the roundhouse taken February 11, 1989. The strange shapes draped around the work area are electrical conduits left suspended when the roof collapsed. Among the identifiable objects in the debris are a drill press, a vertical mill, several copper hydraulic lines, some gauges, and parts of a lathe.   *(©Paul Connor)*

Engines 476 (left) and 473 (right). The 473 in stall number one suffered the worst damage because it was closest to the source of the fire and because the tender was fully loaded with coal, which burned. The steam dome was damaged, and the cab was totally destroyed. Engine 473 had been completely overhauled prior to the tragedy and was ready to be fired up.

(Erick Nelson)

Beyond the rubble at the rear of the roundhouse, engine 476 sits, forlorn and forsaken in stall number one. This engine was the first to be returned to service. It made a successful trial run April 13 to Cascade Canyon Wye, pulling seven empty coaches. As this train left Durango, it passed under crossed ladders of Durango Fire Department, a fitting tribute to the importance of the D&SNG to Durango and southwestern Colorado. (©Paul Conner)

Close-up of engine 481 on April 7, 1989. At the time of the fire, 481 had no boiler jacket, lagging, or flues, and both the smokebox front and firebox doors were open, so heat from the fire went completely through the engine. Workers were still replacing the boiler jacket, external fittings and repairing the smokebox. Engine 478, right, looked as if it had just come from the American Locomotive factory.

This view graphically illustrates how much was accomplished in less than two months time. From left to right are engines 481, newly-painted 478, 497, 476 (behind the Pettibone machine), and 480. (Both photos, F.W. Osterwald)

The annual opening day on the narrow gauge is always a special time, but festivities for the May 5–6, 1989 opening, were even more notable because of the Durango roundhouse fire in February 1989. It was with a great sense of relief and gratitude to all employees of the Durango & Silverton Narrow Gauge Railroad that the Durango Chamber of Commerce and other tourism organizations planned "Full Steam Ahead Days" to welcome the return of **The Silverton**.

One highlight of these festivities was the introduction of longtime Silverton Branch conductor Alva Lyons, by master of ceremonies C.W. McCall. Lyons, then 92, worked for the Rio Grande for 51 years and was largely responsible for the campaign to save the Silverton Branch from abandonment. Following his introduction, he gave a long, healthy and very energetic "All 1 1 1 Aboaarrrrd." Lyons passed away in February 1990. On August 3, 1991, a memorial plaque in his honor was unveiled in ceremonies in front of the Durango depot. The plaque states: "In memory of Alva F. Lyons (1897-1990). Conductor, 'The Silverton' His career with the Denver & Rio Grande Western Railroad spanned 51 years from 1915 to 1966. His vision and perseverance were important factors in saving the Silverton Branch from abandonment in the 1950s. He offered coffee, information and tall tales to mid-century tourists, increasing ridership and winning friends from around the world."

Conductor Alva F. Lyons, a railroader who was instrumental in promoting **The Silverton** *as a tourist attraction, never tired of telling passengers of his experiences on the narrow gauge.* (*J.A. Taylor. Collection of the Museum of New Mexico*)

On January 10, 1990, exactly one year after the fire, formal dedication ceremonies were held for a new 36,000-sq ft roundhouse and machine shop complex. Invited guests saw the seven new engine stalls, eight new locomotive storage stalls, and the new machine shop with its 20-ton traveling crane. With a total of 27 new machines, including a Craven quartering machine obtained from the South African Railroad, the D&SNG's shops are now completely self-sufficient. The total cost of the new facilities exceeded $2 million.

These photos, taken from Smelter Mountain in May 1989 (top) and May 1990 (bottom), document the dramatic changes in the Durango yards in one year.
(Both photos, Ed Boucher, courtesy D&SNG Railroad)

157

The infamous Snowshed slide at mile 492.5 did its usual job of making the work of opening the line to Silverton a real challenge in 1995. This dramatic southward view was taken while D&SNG crews, using front end loaders, removed snow from the track. Contrast this operation with that used in 1905-06 as shown on pp. 133-134.

(Andrew Councill, Durango Herald)

Amos Cordova Retires

When the D&RGW transferred Amos Cordova to Durango to become station agent in 1962, little did he know that he would play an important part in the incredible changes and growth of The Silverton during the next 37 years. In 1962, after the Interstate Commerce Commission (ICC) ruled the line could not be abandoned as it "serves a public need," the D&RGW embarked on an extensive rebuilding and restoration program for the railroad and the Durango depot area. Under the direction of Alexis McKinney, newly appointed director of Rio Grande Land, and Amos Cordova, ridership increased and by the mid-1960s, passed the 500,000 mark. In spite of this success, the Rio Grande wanted out of the tourist railroad business and in 1981 sold this last remaining portion of the Rio Grande's narrow gauge system (p. 142) to Charles E. Bradshaw Jr. of Orlando, Fla. With the sale, Amos became vice president of marketing and public relations of the new Durango & Silverton Narrow Gauge Railroad.

When asked if he ever thought **The Silverton** would carry 200,000 passengers in a year, he quickly replied, "I never had any doubt." Amos designed the first logo for the D&SNG. His wife, Julie, also worked for 22 years in the Durango depot as a cashier. Her ready smile and friendliness will be remembered by all who met her at the ticket window.

Cordova said he feels very fortunate to have worked for the railroad for 47 exciting years and made so many friends. A native of Alamosa, he went to work for the D&RGW in 1950 as a student telegrapher at Monte Vista, Colo. In the fall he was sent to Chama, N.M. where he earned his seniority. He was bumped in November 1957 and worked on the extra board as station agent at 24 towns throughout Colorado. The Cordovas will continue to make Durango their home and Amos plans to spend more time on two avocations—painting and photography.

A retirement party was held for Amos and Julie on February 24, 1998 in the Centennial Room of the Strater Hotel with more than a hundred friends and co-workers present. Also in February the Colorado Railroad Museum Historical Foundation voted Amos an Honorary Life Membership. Alexis McKinney, a trustee of the museum for 20 years, summed up Cordova's accomplishments with the following lines:

"Amos Cordova and The Silverton Train"
"The Silverton Train and Amos Cordova"
"Either or both ways, to think of one without the other is—unthinkable! That's how it as been for as long as we can remember, and will remain among all who share the Spirit of Railroading."

EQUIPMENT ROSTER

LOCOMOTIVES

IN SERVICE	YEAR BUILT	YEAR REBUILT
473	1923	D&SNG 1989
476	1923	D&SNG 1989
478	1923	D&SNG 1989
480	1925	D&SNG 1985, 1989
481	1925	D&SNG 1981, 1989
482	1925	D&SNG 1992

NOT IN SERVICE		
42 (ex-D&RG 420; ex-RGS 42)	1887	
493	1902	D&RGW 1928
498	1902	D&RGW 1930
499	1902	D&RGW 1930

PASSENGER AND SPECIAL-USE EQUIPMENT

No.	Name	Present Use	Original Use	Year Built	Year Rebuilt	Use After Rebuild
64	—	Baggage-concession	Mail-baggage 64	D&RG 1889	D&SNG 1984	Concession
126	—	Concession	Baggage no. 27	D&RG 1883	D&RGW 1939	Baggage
					D&RGW 1963	Snack-bar car
					D&RGW 1979	Coach
					D&SNG 1982	Concession
212	—	Concession	Coach 20	D&RG 1879	D&RG 1887	Coach-baggage 215
					D&RGW 1942	Coach-baggage 212
					D&RGW 1964	Snack-bar car
					D&RGW 1979	Coach
					D&SNG 1982	Snack-bar car
					D&SNG 1986	Concession
213	Home Ranch	Handicapped access	Passenger-baggage	D&SNG 1983		
257	Shenandoah	Coach	Coach 43	Jackson & Sharp 1880	D&RG 1886	Coach
					RGS 1891	Coach
					RGS 1920s	Passenger-baggage
					D&SNG 1986	Coach
270	Pinkerton	Coach	Coach 46	Jackson & Sharp 1880	D&RGW 1924	Kitchen-diner outfit
					D&SNG 1982	Coach
291	King Mine	Coach	Coach 67	Jackson & Sharp 1881	D&RGW 1924	Non-revenue work svc.
					D&SNG 1984	Coach
311	McPhee	Coach	Coach 87	Jackson & Sharp 1881	D&SNG 1984	Coach
312	Silverton	Coach	Coach 312	D&RG 1887	D&RGW 1937	First-class coach
					D&RGW 1957	Coach
					D&RGW 1979	Coach
319	Needlton	Coach	Coach 95	Jackson & Sharp 1882	D&RGW 1937	First-class coach
					D&RGW 1957	Coach
					D&RGW 1978	Coach
323	Animas City	Coach	Coach 323	D&RG 1887	D&RGW 1937	First-class coach
					D&RGW 1957	Coach
					D&RGW 1978	Coach
327	Durango	Coach	Coach 327	D&RG 1887	D&RGW 1937	First-class coach
					D&RGW 1957	Coach
					D&RGW 1978	Coach
330	Cascade	Coach	Coach	D&RGW 1963		
331	Trimble	Coach	Coach	D&RGW 1963		
332	La Plata	Coach	Coach	D&RGW 1964		
333	Tacoma	Coach	Coach	D&RGW 1964		
334	Hermosa	Coach	Coach	D&RGW 1964		
335	Elk Park	Coach	Coach	D&RGW 1964		
336	Rockwood	Coach	Coach	D&RGW 1964		
337	San Juan	Coach	Coach	D&RGW 1964		
566	—	Concession	Mail 14	D&RG 1882	D&RG ca. 1888	Excursion car
					D&RG 1914	B&B coach-outfit
					D&SNG 1982	Concession
630	Hunt	Coach	Coach	D&SNG 1984		
631	North Star	Coach	Coach	D&SNG 1985		
632	Tefft	Coach	Coach	D&SNG 1986		

OPEN OBSERVATION CARS

No.	Name	Present Use	Original Use	Year Built	Year Rebuilt	Use After Rebuild
313	—	Open observation	Open obs. 1002	D&SNG 1987-88	D&SNG 1997	Same
400	—	Open observation	S.G. boxcar 67191	Pullman 1916	D&RGW 1953	N.G. pipe gondola 9609
					D&RGW 1963	Open observation
401	—	Open observation	S.G. boxcar 66665	Pullman 1916	D&RGW 1953	N.G. pipe gondola 9611
					D&RGW 1963	Open observation
402	—	Open observation	S.G. boxcar 66271	Pullman 1916	D&RGW 1953	N.G. pipe gondola 9605
					D&RGW 1963	Open observation
403	—	Open observation	S.G. boxcar	Pullman 1916	D&RGW 1953	N.G. pipe gondola 9606
					D&RGW 1964	Open observation
404	—	Open observation	S.G. boxcar	Pullman 1916	D&RGW 1953	N.G. pipe gondola 9600
					D&RGW 1964	Open observation

No.		Type		Builder		Owner/Year	Description
406	—	Open observation	S.G. stock car	1937		D&SNG 1985	Open observation
407	—	Open observation	S.G. stock car	1937		D&SNG 1985	Open observation
408	—	Open observation	S.G. stock car	1937		D&SNG 1986	Open observation
409	—	Open observation	S.G. stock car	1937		D&SNG 1986	Open observation
411	—	Open observation	S.G. boxcar	Pullman 1916		D&RGW 1953?	N.G. pipe gondola 9603
						D&SNG 1982	Partial rebuild to 405
						D&SNG 1985	Open observation
412	—	Open observation	S.G. boxcar	Pullman 1916		D&RGW 1953?	N.G. pipe gondola 9608
						D&SNG 1982	Partial rebuild to 406
						D&SNG 1986	Open observation
413	—	Open observation	S.G. stock car	1937		D&SNG 1983	Open observation
414	—	Open observation	S.G. stock car	1937		D&SNG 1984	Open observation
415	—	Open observation	S.G. stock car	1937		D&SNG 1984	Open observation
416	—	Open observation	S.G. stock car	1937		D&SNG 1989	Open observation

SPECIAL CARS

No.	Name	Type		Builder		Owner/Year	Description
350	Alamosa	Parlor car	Chaircar 25	Jackson & Sharp 1880		D&RG 1919	Office-living car
						D&RGW 1924	Parlor-smoker car
						D&RGW 1937	Parlor-buffet car
						D&RGW 1957	Coach
						D&RGW 1978	Coach
						D&SNG 1981	Parlor car
B-2	Cinco Animas	Private car	Emigrant sleeper 103	D&RG 1883		D&RG 1909	Paycar "F"
						D&RG 1917	Business car B-2
						Private, 1963	Private car
B-3	Nomad	Private car	Chaircar 16	Billmeyer & Small 1878		D&RG 1886	Business car "N"
						D&RG 1917	Officer's sleeping car
						Private, 1957	Private car
						D&SNG 1987	Private car
						D&SNG 1997	Private car
3681	—	RailCamp car	N.G. boxcar 3681	1903 or 1904		D&RGW 1924	Boxcar
						D&SNG 1984	RailCamp car
0500	—	Caboose	Caboose 1	D&RG 1886		D&SNG 1993	Caboose

CARS NOT IN SERVICE

No.	Name	Type		Builder		Owner/Year	Description
460	—	Coach	Emigrant sleeper	D&RG 1886		D&RG 1903	Construction outfit
						D&RG 1914	Kitchen-diner outfit
						D&RGW 1923	Work train outfit
						BHC 1957	Coach
B-7	Gen. Willam Jackson Palmer	Business car	Baggage	D&RG 1880		D&RG 1886	Paycar "R"
						D&RGW 1963	Business car B-7

REFERENCES

GEOLOGY

Atwood, W.W., and Mather, K.F.,1932, Physiography and Quaternary Geology of the San Juan Mountains, Colorado: U.S. Geological Survey Professional Paper 166, 176 p.

Baars, D.L., and Knight, R.L., 1957, Pre-Pennslyvanian Stratigraphy of the San Juan Mountains and Four Corners Area: *in* New Mexico Geological Survey Guidebook, 8th Field Conference, Southwestern San Juan Mountains, Colorado, p. 108-131.

Burbank, W.S., Eckel, E.B., and Varnes, D.J., 1947, The San Juan Region (Colorado): Colorado Mineral Resources Bulletin, p. 396-446.

Cross, Whitman, Howe, Ernest, and Ransome, F.L., 1905, Description of the Silverton Quadrangle, Colorado: U.S. Geological Survey Atlas, Folio 120.

Cross, Whitman, Howe, Ernest, Irving, J.D., and Emmons, W.H., 1905, Description of the Needle Mountains, Quadrangle, Colorado: U.S. Geological Survey Atlas, Folio 131.

Cross, Whitman, and Hole, Allen D., 1910, Description of the Engineer Mountain Quadrangle, Colorado, U.S. Geological Survey Atlas, Folio 171.

Endlich, F.M., 1876, Report (on the San Juan District, Colorado): U.S. Geological Survey of the Territories (Hayden), Annual Report 8, p. 181-240.

Gary, Margaret, McAfee, Robert, Jr., and Wolf, Carol L., editors, 1972, Glossary of Geology: American Geological Institute, Washington, D.C., 805 p.

George, R.D., 1920, Mineral Waters of Colorado: Colorado Geological Survey, Bulletin 11, 474 p.

Henderson, C.W., 1926, Mining in Colorado, a History of Discovery, Development and Production: U.S. Geological Survey Professional Paper 138, 263 p.

Kelley, Vincent, C., 1957, General Geology and Tectonics of the Western San Juan Mountains, Colorado: *in* New Mexico Geological Society Guidebook, 8th Field Conference, Southwestern San Juan Mountains, Colorado, p. 154-162.

——————— , 1957, Vein and Fault Systems of the Western San Juan Mountains Mineral Belt, Colorado: *in* New Mexico Geological Society Guidebook, 8th Field Conference, Southwestern San Juan Mountains, Colorado, p. 173-176.

Kilgore, Lee, W., 1955, Geology of the Durango Area, La Plata County,Colorado: *in* Four Corners Geological Society Guidebook, no. 1, p. 118-124.

Kottlowski, Frank E., 1957, Mesozoic Strata Flanking the Southwestern San Juan Mountains, Colorado and New Mexico: *in* New Mexico Geological Society Guidebook, 8th Field Conference, San Juan Mountains, Colorado, p. 138-153.

Larsen, Esper, S. Jr., and Cross, Whitman, 1956, Geology and Petrology of the San Juan Region, Southwestern Colorado: U.S. Geological Survey, Professional Paper 258, 303 p.

Luedke, Robert G., and Burbank, Wilbur S., 1968, Volcanism and Cauldron Development in the Western San Juan Mountains, Colorado: *in* Quarterly of the Colorado School of Mines, Golden, Colo., v. 63, no. 3, p. 175-208.

Mather, Kirtley, F., 1957, Geomorphology of the San Juan Mountains: *in* New Mexico Geological Society Guidebook, 8th Field Conference, Southwestern San Juan Mountains, Colorado, p. 102-108.

Parker, Sybil P, editor, 1988, McGraw-Hill Encyclopedia of the Geological Sciences, (2d. ed.): McGraw-Hill Book Co., New York, N.Y., 722 p.

Ransome, F.L., 1901, A Report on the Economic Geology of the Silverton Quadrangle, Colorado: U.S. Geological Survey, Bulletin 182, 265 p.

Silver, Caswell, 1957, Silverton to Durango via Railroad: *in* New Mexico Geological Society Guidebook, 8th Field Conference, Southwestern San Juan Mountains, Colorado, p. 75-90.

Stevens, T.A., Schmitt, L.J., Jr., Sheridan, M.J., and Williams, F.E., 1969, Mineral Resources of the San Juan Primitive Area, Colorado: U.S. Geological Survey, Bulletin 1261-F, 187 p.

Stokes, Wm. Lee, and Varnes, David J., 1955, Glossary of Selected Terms: Colorado Scientific Society Proceedings, v. 16, 165 p.

Tewksbury, B.J., 1985, Revised Interpretation of the Ages of Allochthonous Rocks of the Uncompahgre Formation, Needle Mountains, Colorado: Geological Society of America, Bull. v. 96, p. 224-232.

Varnes, David, J. 1963, Geology and Ore Deposits of the South Silverton Mining Area, San Juan County, Colorado: U.S. Geological Survey, Professional Paper 378-A, 47 p.

Wengerd, Sherman A., and Baars, Donald L., 1957, Durango to Silverton Road Log: *in* New Mexico Geological Society Guidebook, 8th Field Conference, Southwestern San Juan Mountains, Colorado, p. 39-51.

Wengerd, Sherman, A., 1957, Permo-Pennslvanian Strata of the San Juan Mountains, Colorado: *in* New Mexico Geological Society Guidebook, 8th Field Conference, Southwestern San Juan Mountains, Colorado, p. 131-138.

Zapp, A.D., 1949, Geology and Coal Resources of the Durango Area, La Plata and Montezuma Counties, Colorado: U.S. Geological Survey Oil and Gas Investigations Preliminary Map 109.

HISTORY

Ayers, Mary C., 1951, Howardsville in the San Juan: The Colorado Magazine, v. XXVIII, no. 4.

Bartlett, Richard A., 1962, Great Surveys of the West: University of Oklahoma Press, Norman, Okla., 410 p.

Bauer, William H., Ozment, James L., and Willard, John H., 1990, Colorado Post Offices, 1859-1989: Colorado Railroad Museum, Golden, Colorado, 280 p.

Bear, Leith Lende, 1985, Trimble Hot Springs, a Historical Tale: Trimble Hot Springs Inc., Durango, Colorado, 40 p.

Bender, Norman J., 1964, History of the Durango Area: *in* Four Corners Geological Society, Durango-Silverton Guidebook, p. 18-29.

Bird, Allan G., 1986, Silverton Gold, The Story of Silverton's Largest Gold Mine: Silverton, Colorado, 152 p.

Darley, George M., 1899, Pioneering in the San Juan: Chicago, Ill.

Hall, Frank, 1895, History of the State of Colorado: v. IV, Chicago, Ill.

Ingersoll, Ernest, 1882, Silvery San Juan: in Harpers Magazine, v. LXIV, no. 383, p. 689-704.

——————— , 1888, The Crest of the Continent: R.R. Donnelley, Chicago, Ill., 344 p.

Kaplan, Michael, 1982, Otto Mears, Paradoxical Pathfinder: San Juan Book Co., Silverton, Colo., 284 p.

Logan, Kenneth, T., 1962, The History of La Plata County: *in* The Encyclopedia of Colorado, Colorado Historical Association, p. 278-282.

Marshall, John B., 1962, History of San Juan County: *in* San Juan County. The Encyclopedia of Colorado, Colorado Historical Association, p. 311-316.

Newhall, Beaumont, and Edkins, Diana, E., 1974, William H. Jackson: Morgan and Morgan, Amon Carter Museum, Ft. Worth, Tex., 158 p.

Nossaman, Allen, Many More Mountains, v. I, Silverton's Roots: Sundance Ltd., Denver, Colo., 352 p.

——————— , 1993, Many More Mountains, v. II, Ruts to Silverton: Sundance Ltd., Denver, Colo., 352 p.

——————— , 1993, Silverton's Story: *in* All Aboard, D&SNG Magazine, Starlight Publishing Co., Albuquerque, New Mex., p. 13-16.

Olsen, Mary Ann, 1962, The Silverton Story: Bearber Printing Co., Cortez, Colo., 28 p.

Pinkert, Leta, 1964, True Stories of Early Days in the San Juan Basin: Hustler Press, Inc., Farmington, New Mex., 38 p.

Sarah Platt Decker Chapter, N.S.D.A.R. 1942, 1946, 1952, 1961, Pioneers of the San Juan Country: v. I and II, Out West Printing Co., v. III, Durango Printing Co., v. IV, Big Mountain Press [all volumes bound together].

Silver, Caswell, 1957, History and Folklore of the San Juan Region: *in* New Mexico Geological Society Guidebook, 8th Field Conference, Southwestern San Juan Mountains, Colorado, p. 222-234.

Smith, Duane A., 1980, Rocky Mountain Boom Town, A History of Durango: University of New Mexico Press, Albuquerque, New Mex., 214 p.

——————— , 1992, Rocky Mountain Mining Camps, The Urban Frontier: University Press of Colorado, Niwot, Colo., 304 p.

——————— , Durango Lore: in All Aboard, D&SNG Magazine, v. 2, no. 1, Starlight Publishing Co., Albuquerque, New Mex., p. 9-10.

Thompson, Ian, 1964, The Silverton Country. A Historical Sketch: *in* Four Corners Geological Society, Durango-Silverton Guidebook, p. 1-5.

RAILROADS
Anonymous, 1883, Official Railway Guide to Colorado, the East and West: Reprinted 1978 by Mobile Post Office Society, Omaha, Neb. 120 p.
_____ , 1951-1995, Iron Horse News: newsletter of the Colorado Railroad Museum, Golden, Colo.
_____ , 1953, Ghost town and Calico Railway: Ghost Town, Calif., 59 p.
_____ , The Silverton and Rio Grande-Land: *in* Colorado Annual, 1963, Colorado Railroad Museum, Golden, Colo.,15 p.
_____ , 1964, Along the Narrow Gauge: U.S. Forest Service pamphlet.
_____ , To Silverton in Snow: *in* Colorado Annual, 1964, Colorado Railroad Museum, Golden, Colo., 15 p.
_____ , Locomotives of the Rio Grande: 1980, Colorado Railroad Museum, Golden, Colo., 96 p.
Athearn, Robert G., 1962, Rebel in the Rockies: Yale University Press, New Haven, Conn., 395 p.
Beebe, Lucius, and Clegg, Charles, 1958, Narrow Gauge in the Rockies: Howell-North, Berkeley, Calif., 224 p.
_____ , 1962, Rio Grande, Mainline of the Rockies: Howell-North, Berkeley, Calif., 380 p.
Carter, Kenneth, E., 1964, The Narrow Gauge Lines: *in* Four Corners Geological Society, Durango-Silverton Guidebook, p. 7-17.
Chappell, Gordon, S., 1971, Logging Along the Denver & Rio Grande: Colorado Railroad Museum, Golden, Colo., 190 p.
Choda, Kelly, 1956, Thirty Pound Rails: The Filter Press, Aurora, Colo., 46 p.
Crum, Josie M., 1956, Rails Among the Peaks, The D&RG in the San Juan Mountains: reprinted from Railway and Locomotive Historical Society, Bulletin no. 76.
Crum, Josie, Moore, 1961, The Rio Grande Southern Railroad: Hamilton Press, Inc., Durango, Colo., 431 p.
Denver & Rio Grande Railroad records and photographs from 1871 to present: Library, Colorado Historical Society, Denver, Colo.
Dorman, Richard L., 1987, Durango Always a Railroad Town, v. II: R.D. Publications, Inc., Santa Fe, New Mex., 184 p.
Ferrell, Mallory Hope, 1973, Silver San Juan, The Rio Grande Southern Railroad: Pruett Publishing Co., Boulder, Colo., 643 p.
Hauck, Cornelius, W., and Richardson, Robert W., 1963, Steam in the Rockies, a Denver & Rio Grande Roster: Colorado Railroad Museum, Golden, Colo., 32 p.
Hungerford, John B., 1955, Narrow Gauge to Silverton: Hungerford Press, Reseda, Calif., 36 p.
Hunt, Louie, 1955, The Silverton Train: Leucadia, Calif.
LeMassena, R.A., 1964, Colorado's Mountain Railroads, v. III: Smoking Stack Press, Golden, Colo.
_____ , 1974, Rio Grande to the Pacific: Sundance Ltd., Denver, Colo., 416 p.
McCoy, Dell and Collman, Russ, 1971, The Rio Grande Pictorial 1871-1971: Sundance Ltd., Denver, Colo., 216 p.
McKinney, Alexis, 1979, The Silverton's Three Private Cars, Legends on Rails: *in* Colorado Rail Annual no. 14, Colorado Railroad Museum, Golden, Col., p. 9-23.
Ormes, Robert M., 1963, Railroads and the Rockies: Sage Books, Denver, Colo., 406 p.
Osterwald, Doris, B., 1991, High Line to Leadville: Western Guideways, Ltd., Lakewood, Colo., 160 p.
_____ , 1992, Ticket to Toltec (2nd. ed.): Western Guideways, Ltd., Lakewood, Colo.,128 p.
_____ , 1994, Beyond the Third Rail with Monte Ballough and His Camera: Western Guideways, Ltd., Lakewood, Colo., 204 p.
Richardson, Robert W., 1994, Narrow Gauge News: Colorado Railroad Museum, Colorado Rail Annual No. 21, Golden, Colo., 303 p.
Richardson, Robert W., Walker, John S., Jr., and Farewell, R.C., 1991, A Silverton Trilogy: *in* Coal, Cinders and Parlor Cars: A Century of Colorado Passenger Trains, Colorado Rail Annual No. 19, Railroad Museum, Golden, Colo., 238 p.
Sloan, Robert E., and Skowronski, Carl A., The Rainbow Route, an Illustrated History: Sundance, Ltd., Denver, Colo., 416 p.
Thode, Jackson, C., 1971, A Century of Passenger Trains: *in* The 1970 Denver Westerners Brand Book, The Westerners, Denver, Colo., p. 83-265.
_____ , 1989, George L. Beam and the Denver & Rio Grande: v. II: Sundance Ltd., Denver, Colo., 280 p.

NATURE
Baerg, Harry J., 1955, How to Know the Western Trees: Wm. C. Brown Co., Dubuque, Iowa, 170 p.
Craighead, John J., Craighead, Frank C. Jr., and Davis, Ray J., 1991, A Field Guide to Rocky Mountain Wildflowers: Houghton Mifflin Co., Boston, Mass. 275 p.
Pesman, Walter M., 1988, Meet the Natives (8th ed.): Denver Botanic Gardens, Denver, Colo., 237 p.
Peterson, Roger Tory, 1990, A Field Guide to Western Birds (3rd. ed): Houghton Mifflin Co., Boston, N.Y., 432 p.
Robbins, Chandler S., Robbins, Bertel Bruun, and Zim, Herbert S., 1966, A Guide to Field Identification Birds of North American: Golden Press, New York, N.Y., 340 p.
Wassink, Jan L., 1993, Mammals of the Central Rockies: Mountain Press Publishing Co., Missouli, Mont., 162 p.
Watts, Tom, 1972, Rocky Mountain Tree Finder: Nature Study Guild, Rochester, N.Y., 62 p.
Weber, William A., 1976, Rocky Mountain Flora: Colorado Associated University Press, Boulder, Colo., 479 p.
Whitley, Stephan, 1985, Western Forests: Alfred Knopf, Inc., New York, N.Y., 670 p.
Yocom, Charles, Weber, William, Beidleman, Richard, and Malick, Donald, 1969, Wildlife and Plants of the Southern Rocky Mountains, Naturegraph Company, Hearldsburg, Calif., 132 p.

NEWPAPERS
Alamosa Journal
Colorado Chieftan, Pueblo
Colorado Springs Gazette
Denver Post
Denver Republican
Denver Tribune
Durango Democrat
Durango Evening Herald
Durango Daily Herald
Durango Herald
Durango Idea
Durango Record
Durango Southwest
La Plata Miner, Silverton
The Silverton Standard and the Miner
Ouray Times
San Luis Valley Courier, Alamosa
The Southwest, Animas City

SOURCES FOR GUIDE MAPS
U.S.Geological Survey 72° quadrangle maps
The geology was compiled from the following maps and supplemented with personal field work:
U.S. Geological Survey, Folios, 120, 131, 171; Professional Papers 258, Plate I, 378-A, Plate I:, Oil & Gas Investigations, Preliminary Map 109.
Four Corners Geological Society, Durango-Silverton Guidebook, p. 67-71.

INDEX

Numbers in boldface are photographs